THE SURFACE DESIGNER'S ART

THE SURFACE DESIGNER'S ART

CONTEMPORARY FABRIC PRINTERS PAINTERS AND DYERS

Lark Books

INTRODUCTION BY
KATHERINE WESTPHAL

Published in 1993 by Lark Books
50 College Street
Asheville, North Carolina, U.S.A. 28801
Copyright © 1993, Lark Books

Art Director: Chris Colando
Editor: Nancy Orban
Production: Elaine Thompson, Chris Colando

Library of Congress Cataloging-in-Publication Data

The surface designer's art / introduction by Katherine Westphal.
     p.   cm.
    Includes bibliographical references and index.
    ISBN 0-937274-67-4 :
    1. Textile design--History--20th century.   2. Textile fabrics--
History--20th century.   3. Textile designers--Philosophy.
I. Westphal, Katherine.
NK9500.S87   1993
746.6--dc20   92-42334
                                              CIP

First Edition

Cover: Mary Anne Jordan's **Squares in Squares or Wigs & Wheat** (detail).
Screen print, arashi shibori, direct dye, appliqué, and embroidery on cotton.
Full piece 43 by 43 inches. Photo: Luke S. Jordan.

Printed by Oceanic Graphic Printing in Hong Kong

ISBN 0-937274-67-4

TABLE OF CONTENTS

FOREWORD: INFLUENCES FROM THE PAST

Decorating fabric by hand application of designs using dye or pigment—surface design—has been going on for centuries. But not until recently has the history of the embellishment of fabric begun to be sorted out.

From the chaos that exists in centuries-old digs, archaeologists attempt to create some order. In the past, they ignored the remnants of cloth which survived the elements in favor of more substantial items like pottery, tools, and jewels. In recent times, though, textiles have been considered just as fundamental to knowing a culture as other recovered materials. A few notable finds allow us tantalizing glimpses of the origins of color and pattern used by today's surface design artists.

COLOR

In 1962 archaeologist James Mellaart was excavating the sixth level of a dig at Catal Huyuk in present-day Turkey. Under thousands of years of dust and rubble, he found a group of beads. That in itself was not significant; beads had already

6

PAINTED LINEN SHROUD. THE COMBINATION OF REPEAT, REVERSE, AND ZIGZAG PATTERNING WITH FIGURATIVE DRAWING IS A FINE EXAMPLE OF ANCIENT SURFACE DESIGN. FUNERARY SHROUD. EGYPTIAN PTOLEMAIC PERIOD (305–30 B.C.). PHOTO: COURTESY THE BROOKLYN MUSEUM; 37.1811E, CHARLES EDWIN WILBOUR FUND.

been unearthed at several ancient sites in Switzerland, in Holland, and around the Aegean Sea. But these beads were different. Inside the string holes were traces of red—strong evidence that the beads had once been strung on red thread. Dated at 6000 B.C., the beads proved to be the earliest finds of colored fiber. The paleobotanist working with Mellaart speculated that red ocher, plentiful in the region, had supplied the pigment.

Other evidence from later sites in the Middle East and Mongolia tells us that, not surprisingly, colored textiles were used primarily as clothing and as ornaments for the body. Since there is no evidence as to exactly when or where dyeing of textiles began, or precisely how it originated, we are all free to speculate.

It is easy to imagine how our ancestors might have stumbled upon the natural dyes themselves. The blue from indigo and woad might have appeared when leaves of these plants toppled into sun-drenched puddles of water and, after awhile, produced an interesting blue scum. The red from madder root was within easy reach of people who survived partly by digging, pounding, and cooking all manner of tubers and roots. A careful observer might have noticed that the dried bodies of dead insects—kermes and cochineal—blazed scarlet when stepped upon. And in disposing of the remains of last night's seafood dinner, a keen-eyed cook might have discovered murex purple.

How primitive peoples discovered mordants—substances that make dyed cloth colorfast—is harder to fathom. True, the common mordants found in ancient dyed cloths were all close at hand: aluminum salts are present in tea leaves; tannin is found in acorns and the bark of oak, hemlock, and willow trees; and ammonia is abundant in urine. By what happy accident someone learned to add these substances to the dyepot is anyone's guess.

P A T T E R N / D E S I G N

The origins of pattern in textiles are equally obscure. Applying wax, vegetable pastes, or mud to block out dye and thus create patterns may have begun concurrently in Asia, India, and Africa.

At least we know that the practice is old. Patterned textiles are known to have existed around 2000 B.C. A wall painting from this period, found in the tomb of a high-ranking Egyptian official, shows a group of women in patterned garments. Frescoes, figurines, and vases of the same period from the Mediterranean islands of Crete, Thira, and Melos depict women wearing sophisticated patterned clothing. Dye resist techniques clearly were being used.

In another region, a woolen piece decorated with plants and human figures was found in a fourth-century-B.C. tomb near Kertch in what is now Ukraine. Boasting three different colors—black, red, and buff—it was presumably resist-dyed in a multi-step process, with wax or a similar substance blocking out the dye.

Through the ages, artisans have developed a variety of sophisticated techniques to add color and pattern to fabric.

Batik

If wax is melted, it can be painted on fabric with just about anything it will adhere to—a stick, a leaf, a tough blade of grass. Allowed to cool and harden, wax effectively blocks dye wherever it has been applied, thus allowing the dyer to create patterns on the fabric.

Batik reached its highest development on the Indonesian island of Java, which gave the technique its name (batik means "wax writing"). For Javanese artisans, cotton has always been the fabric of choice, even though its stiff fibers require more preparation than do those of linen. Batik also has a long history in China, Egypt, India, Southeast Asia (Thailand, Laos, Vietnam), Japan, and Peru.

Traditional methods still survive. Cloths are hung on frames and the designs applied with pencil or charcoal; often, a stencil is used to outline a pattern. Hot, liquid wax is applied and allowed to cool and harden. Then the cloth is dyed in a cold water bath and allowed to dry. The wax is scraped or boiled off, the cloth is dried, and more hot wax is applied, if multiple colors are desired. In one of those wonderful accidents of artistry, the design caused by the crackle at the edge of the wax, which allows seepage of dye, has been incorporated as a trademark of the process. Artisans in various countries have devised different ways to make this charming soft edge on designed fabric.

Tie-Dye

Less cumbersome than batik, tie-dye has become a mainstream technique in western societies. There is no proof as to where it originated—scholars speculate Persia, China, India, or Turkey—but tie-dye is a modern takeoff of Japanese shibori techniques which are known to have existed in seventh century Japan.

In tie-dye, sections of cloth are folded, pleated, knotted, and/or tied off to prevent the dye from reaching them. There are many traditional variations. The cloth can be wrapped around a pole, bound with string, and compressed to one end of the pole. In a different process, the cloth can be repeatedly reverse-folded, placed between rigid, impermeable covers, and the resulting bundle tied tightly. Using stitching to gather and tie cloth before dyeing offers almost endless design possibilities: loose or close stitch, straight or curved stitching lines, simple or intricate placement of stitches.

Printing

Proof as to when or where block printing, stamping, and stencilling began is not definitive. Small clay stamps have been found in many digs from Neolithic Europe (4000-2500 B.C.) and wooden blocks from sites in India (3000 B.C.), but no fabric has been found with them to substantiate their use on textiles.

Whenever printing techniques developed, it's easy to speculate about the motivation for inventing them. Traditional resist-dyeing methods were somewhat time-consuming. It is fair to assume that, once decorative textiles were developed, the demand for them would have been immediate and extensive. It is also fair to imagine that clever artisans of ancient times began devising time-saving processes to meet the demand.

Screen printing is merely stencilling refined. In the early 1900s, when the process was patented, the design stencil was bonded to the screen and a pigment was passed over it to make a print. Variations of the technique have multiplied rapidly: painting the design directly on the screen with a liquid blockout; covering the entire screen with a water-soluble glue and removing some areas with a solvent; and photographic screen printing, the process allowing for the greatest variety, detail, and room for spontaneity. Whether the design screen is made by applying a light-sensitive coating or by using a light-sensitive film, this process is the fastest yet available.

The creative techniques from the past have been assimilated. Each has led to the development of new fibers, dyes, and techniques. Today's artists have a multitude of techniques at their disposal, including direct painting and dyeing, marbling, cyanotype, and heat transfer of images. They use the techniques liberally. Some concentrate on a single technique; other artists combine, cross over, embellish, and invent. Today's artists stretch beyond the limitations of technique, of materials, of the past. They test the dynamics of order and even flirt with chaos.

A CONTEMPORARY HISTORY: SURFACE DESIGN TODAY

KATHERINE WESTPHAL

Surface design is a pattern willfully executed on a fibrous surface. It is about color—not only the rainbow of colors, but white on white, black on black, and all the shades of grey. In the early 1950s when I began doing surface design, then called printed textiles or fabric decoration, there were rules. Printed textiles were printed. They were in repeat, straight or half drop, three yards long, at least thirty-five inches wide, and the ends were neatly hemmed for exhibition. Accepted techniques were block print, linoleum, wood or potato print, small silkscreen or wax batik. The fabric was stiff with pigment, or the color evasive and fading with cold water dyes. It was an attempt to emulate the industrial roller print fabrics. The goal was to design for the textile industry. You learned the rules and tried to conform to the neat and tidy, clean mechanical look.

Today there are no boundaries, no rules. In 1992 the Museum of Modern Art in New York showed "Allegories of Modernism," an exhibition of contemporary drawing. It became a revelation to see that the old parameters of drawing had fallen. To viewers who had preconceived or traditional ideas of drawing, the show was a disaster. It refuted their touch with reality; it broke the rules. My view of the show was delight. It made anything possible. Drawing could be anything as long as it was personal in viewpoint, and as long as the artist said it was a drawing. Artists make the decisions. If we say it is art, it is art; if we say it is a basket, it is a basket; if we say it is surface design, it is surface design.

Even so, these are questions I asked myself: Can surface design be defined by technique? Can you learn to be a surface designer in school? Is it abstract, non-objective, conceptual, or narrative? Is the message important? Who are the surface designers who have changed my way of thinking?

My first experience with printing textiles came with Mary Dumas, a friend from the 1940s when we were painting majors at the University of California at Berkeley. In the 1950s she was teaching in the Decorative Arts Department at Berkeley. She knew some of the hand printing techniques; I learned from her. We leaned heavily on the Lowie Museum of Anthropology. We experienced African textiles from the research materials of William Bascom, the anthropologist who brought a collection of textiles from Nigeria. It included many lengths of indigo cloth used for native clothing and purchased in the markets, but it also included samples tied but not dyed, as well as tied and dyed and not yet untied.

11

It revealed the process. It also revealed that a textile could be flat or three-dimensional. Function was no longer the criterion for a printed textile. At the same time, Berkeley had a collection of textiles that taught us about the processes of India, Indonesia, and fabric designer/wizard Mariano Fortuny of Italy.

The mid-1960s brought changes in thought, behavior, technical achievements, and an expanding global awareness. There was a revolution among the young. It was an age of defying convention, shocking the establishment. Categories and rules were meant to be tested, to be broken. The flower children broke the rules of personal adornment—a primary use of textiles.

> Tie-dye was in
> Day-glo paint was in
> Rags and patches and holes were in
> Beads, fringes, flowers
> Ethnic clothes and flea market finds
> A total break with tradition.

The artists experienced, observed and acted. We studied, we read, we were aware of what was occurring in the "fine arts" world, and we traveled.

India, with a rich history of printed, dyed and embroidered textiles, became a major influence. Through a program for graduate students sponsored by the Indian government, textile students were able to absorb the lifestyle and textiles. Japan's textile tradition of producing a variety of shibori-decorated fabrics was also influential.

Yoshiko Wada came to the United States from Japan to attend college, bringing with her the traditional fiber aesthetic. She knew the disciplines of shibori and katagami; she knew the secrets of the indigo vat. She shared this magic. In the 1970s, Wada taught the traditional textile techniques of Japanese dyeing in workshops throughout the United States. I participated in one of those workshops in Berkeley. This group of workshop students experienced a fellowship, a sort of family, with a blue tinge on our hands and needle pricks in our fingers. We learned the disciplines of folding and stitching for traditional patterns, and the processes of indigo vat dyeing. We were exposed to the insight of Japanese thought and culture.

The skill of Japanese shibori has led western artists to Japan to explore traditional printing and dyeing techniques. They learn and modify. Each western artist creates an individual imprint far from the Japanese original. The technique has been modified: The dye often is not the traditional indigo, but the more vibrant or somber colors of commercial dyes; the fabrics change from silk to sheerest cotton, polyester, jacquards, and pile. The combination of fabric, dye, and process lends a new meaning to traditional shibori.

Many possibilities for observing textile production were created for me as part of a sabbatical leave program in the University of California system. Every two and a half years, my husband Ed Rossbach and I took off to the other side of the world to see how textiles were produced. We shared these experiences with our students.

I remember our trip to Isfahan, Iran most vividly. I wanted to see the Masid-i-Shah Mosque. It still haunts me over twenty years later. The softly glistening patterned walls, quiet with the stillness and tranquility of a sacred place. There were open, flat courtyards with fountains, a few robed and turbaned holy men walking slowly to the towering arched and domed mosque, then stepping inside to blueness. The entire interior was patterned with flowers and inscriptions from the Koran. The only light came through the perforations of high up arched windows. Blueness and patterns were everywhere.

Later we wandered to the market section. In our explorations for merchandise, we entered a central courtyard. It was an open-air factory, the production area for the dyers and printers. It was crowded with activity. Men everywhere dipping, moving, folding. Huge dye vats in the center. Poles and scaffolds looped with yarns suspended from the roofs. Neatly folded lengths of off-white cloth were piled around the edges. The cloth was saturated with mordant.

Surrounding the courtyard were tiny open-front rooms, dark as caves. Inside, men were printing the textiles, one block print at a time. They sat on the ground at a small padded table less than a foot high, a flat round tray filled with a felt pad saturated with a slightly brownish liquid. A variety of blocks were in the niches in a plastered wall behind them. They selected a block, dipped it into the tray, and carefully positioned it by eye. With a slap of the other well-wrapped and padded arm, a pale imprint was left on the fabric. This process was repeated again and again until the cloth was covered with images. Others took the printed fabric to the central area to dry, and then to the vats where it was submerged into a dye bath. It was dried again, then washed to reveal a bold pattern of brownish red and black. Blue and yellow dyes were then printed onto the patterned cloth. The printed textile we watched being produced was narrative—"The Story of the Rubaiyat of Omar Khayyam." Later I found a bedspread from that workshop in our collection. Today it protects my color photocopier from dust.

All of us find value in these kinds of experiences. We learn from them and we learn from the visions of other contemporary artists. In the early 1950s, Robert Rauschenberg was using the frottage method of rubbing a newspaper image into a surface; it produced a ghostly image which connected ideas together spatially, not statically. The interpretation was flexible, a message between artist and viewer; it meant different things to different people. Pop artist Andy Warhol was another profound influence. His serial images via photo silkscreen became linear in structure, one image following another, frozen in time. Often there was a color change in the image. The repetition heightened the impact. The grid prevailed like a strip of movie film. More artists were discovering alternative uses for the photographic serial image, distorting the image with the machine or printing it on surfaces other than photographic paper. In the mid-1970s, Sonia Sheridan produced textiles that were revolutionary in concept. Experiments with color machine imaging systems allowed her to print serial images without the use of a camera or photo silkscreen. With the 3M color machines, she was able to create generations of images on paper matrices which were transferred onto fabric with a heat press.

Many artists have changed my ideas about surface design, technically and otherwise. I think of Frances Butler and her approach to screen printed fabrics. In the '70s I visited her "Good Stuffs" studio in Emeryville, California, the second floor of a warehouse. It was factory dimensions and the screens were huge; everything was large. The screens extended the entire width of a fifty-inch fabric. The screen itself

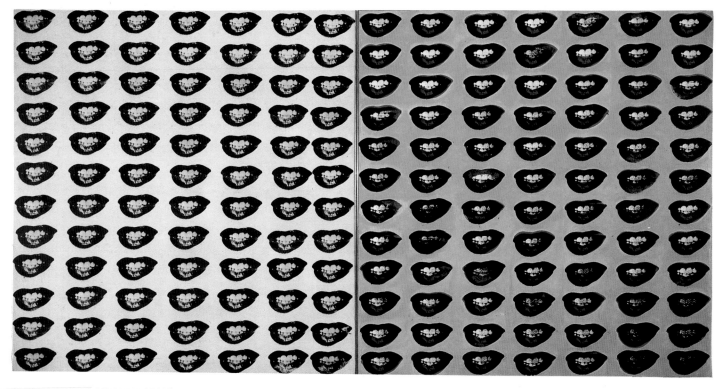

ANDY WARHOL'S SERIAL IMAGES WERE AN INFLUENCE ON TODAY'S SURFACE DESIGNERS. **MARILYN MONROE'S LIPS**, 1962. PHOTO: LEE STALSWORTH, COURTESY OF HIRSHHORN MUSEUM AND SCULPTURE GARDEN, SMITHSONIAN INSTITUTION, GIFT OF JOSEPH H. HIRSHHORN, 1972.

was about five by six feet. No more itsy-bitsy images endlessly linked together. Size changed the nature of the design. It was narrative, not linear as the Bayeux Tapestry, but a juxtaposition of images, small and large, recording the personal vision of Frances Butler. These works were not thought of as painting or drapery yardage, but as components for other objects—garments, cushions, elements for sculpture—all the stuff of her fantastic personal and highly inventive imagination.

In opposition to these large works are the tiny screen images of K. Lee Manuel; a multitude of feathers four inches long, screen printed and hand painted. On a trip to Japan, she discovered a screen printing device, tiny and complete as an audio cassette player. This Japanese screen print machine enables you to expose a four- by five-inch cardboard mounted screen from a black and white photocopy, to ink the screen, and begin printing in less than five minutes. Just lift and press. There is no squeegee and no messy cleanup.

There are endless variations of screen printing. Glen Kaufman, in his work of the '90s, is printing on patterned damask obi silk. The colors are dark and somber to contrast with the applied metal leaf. The photo images are narrative and personal, reflecting his love for Japan. By using two highly prized materials, woven silk and precious metals, he denies their preciousness with a photo of mundane everyday life.

Neda Al-Hilali does non-objective surface design. It is color and texture and spatial movement. She paints and layers paper, cuts or tears it, reassembles it, and, with pressure, fuses it into a single surface. Jason Pollen collages in a different way: the printed and dyed silks have an industrial heat and pressure sensitive interfacing. The fabrics are cut into a multitude of tiny pieces, assembled in a new order, and fused with pressure and heat into a single surface. The textiles are explosive in nature, jewel-like in color.

Ed Rossbach uses the formality of the grid. For example, he uses a simple one- by one-inch piece of scrap lumber and prints a three yard length of cotton satin. Each print is pure color dye. The wood block is printed over and over until a shimmering surface of tiny irregular images is achieved. The process takes days. The dedication to a single length of cloth is enormous. Arturo Alonzo Sandoval also uses the grid, but he uses film strips and Mylar and packaging materials, and fabric interlaced with images and color and texture until he has a reflective and vibrating surface. The layering creates depth, and the fractured images speak a message of today.

A phenomenon of our time is the message T-shirt. It occurs in Africa, Asia, Europe, North America, in fact, everywhere. Wearing it makes a statement. The message or belief is presented not only in words but also in visual images. Causes, political issues, even heroes or cult figures can be given homage. The message is all, and yet the wearer is often not aware of its meaning. The electronic explosion has produced a popular attraction at street fairs: a T-shirt printed with the face of the purchaser. A computer scans the face, prints it on a matrix in full color, then prints it on the T-shirt in less than thirty minutes. A souvenir of a moment in time.

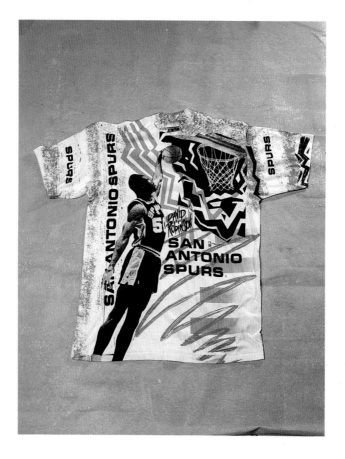

Perhaps the T-shirt has had an influence. Narrative imagery is popular and permissible. Frequently, the commercial world makes decisions for artists. Will it sell? Can it be exhibited? Today, much of surface design is very personal, produced for the artist alone. These designs are frequently autobiographical, telling stories of family history, travel adventures, or pure myth. They may be realistic or lean heavily on surrealism. Each has an individual story.

THE COLOR SHAPES OF CORNELIA BREITENBACH'S PRINTED FABRIC ARE NON-OBJECTIVE, INTERLOCKING LIKE AN INTARSIA MOSAIC. THE FLAT PATTERN WAS TRANSFERRED INTO OPTICAL THREE DIMENSIONS BY SKILLFUL USE OF THE AIRBRUSH. **STROUT**; SILKSCREEN PRINT, AIRBRUSH ON COTTON VELVETEEN; 72 BY 96 INCHES.

New dyes have changed the look of contemporary textiles as have other products: the paste and polymer resists, blue and brown photo printing methods, transfer dyes and crayon, color copy machine transfers, the airbrush, the heat transfer press, and the tiny Japanese screen print machine. It is no longer necessary to limit one-self to traditional methods or materials. Anything goes—paint with acrylic, draw with a marker, embellish with beads and glitter, cut, paste, bond. The surface can be flat or three dimensional; the size, monumental or small enough to fit in the hand. Imagination rules.

Over the years I have seen the work of many surface designers at exhibitions, in magazines, books, slides, and at conferences—and I have had actual contact with a few. There are many dedicated artists working with passion and commitment, exploring ideas, modifying and expanding old techniques, discovering new technologies. They are redefining the boundaries. For each artist mentioned or exhibited, there are hundreds working. I wish we could have a visual record of them all. We all learn from each other, visually from our work, and from the way we speak about it.

Today the whole look of surface design is varied. It is exciting and seems to be the one art form where it is acceptable to be non-objective or abstract, traditional or personal. You can explore a grid, a square, an explosion, or your dream fantasy. It is the freedom for which we all search. ■

C L A R E
V E R S T E G E N

The visual movement and rhythm created by viewing images in repeat was the initial impetus for my interest in printing on fabric. My early works are an exploration of color, texture, shape, and form, and how these elements interact to structure pattern on cloth. I liked the process and the material, the length of cloth being the logical surface for the repetition I was compelled to produce.

I am attracted to the order, arrangement, layers, stacks, bundles, and accumulation of similar shapes or forms: pattern is an important element of my world. A significant aspect of the versatile nature of pattern is its ability to exist both as a surface and a physical structure. I often view piles of firewood, gravel pathways, rippling water, rows of vegetables, crowded parking lots, or architectural exteriors as enormous textiles.

The strength and energy found in multiplicity is one notion I wish to convey when inventing and incorporating pattern. The screen printed fabrics I make focus on the development of pattern as a camouflaged field of information. Camouflage allows animals to be concealed through protective coloration, disguised as distasteful plants or animals, and hidden in sunlight or shadow. The effect of camouflage in altering visual perception is the basis for my conceptual and formal investigations.

ESCAPE FROM THE BLUE BOX SYNDROME, 1984; COTTON; SCREEN PRINT; 96 BY 45 INCHES.

The interruptions of a repeated motif through the discovery of unexpected images intensify the level of retrieving layers of printed information. Disguised surfaces exist within the printed texture of rocks and stones on a cloth which inherently possesses the qualities of pliability and lightness.

Teetering between obscure and distinct images, implied and actual surfaces, the viewer could possibly overlook the undercover layers of printed, disparate images. Visual puns play hide-and-seek games, as the use of pattern reflects the notion of scanning or retracing a visual path, in the process of searching and finding. Measuring devices serve as a metaphor to gauge the distance between reality and illusion, and as reflections of personal systems used to evaluate and make judgments in daily life.

A SERIES OF FROZEN TEXTILES WERE FOUND IN SOME LATE FIFTH-CENTURY B.C. TOMBS OF CENTRAL ASIATIC HERDSMEN. ROBBERS OF ANTIQUITY DUG INTO THE TOMBS. OVER THE CENTURIES, WATER POURED IN, GRADUALLY FILLING EACH ONE AND THE AREA AROUND IT WITH LAYERED ICE. USING BUCKETS OF HOT WATER, ARCHAEOLOGISTS DESCENDED LAYER BY LAYER UNTIL THE CONTENTS WERE REVEALED.

BLIND DIFFERENCE, 1992;
LAYERED COTTON; SCREEN
PRINT; 55 BY 45 INCHES.

SAW IT, 1990; COTTON; SCREEN PRINT; 56 BY 90 INCHES. PHOTO: TOM NEFF.

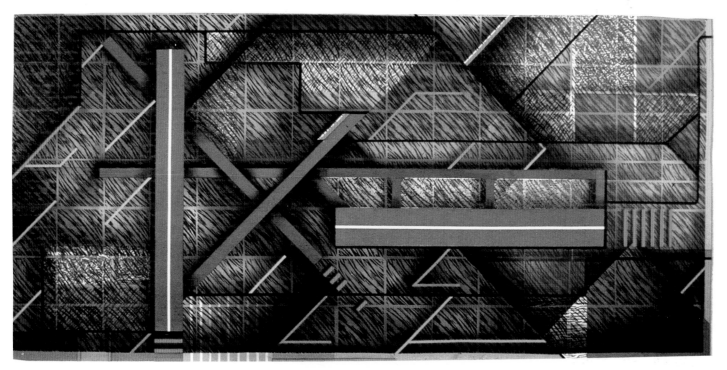

INTERSECTING PLANES, 1987; COTTON; SCREEN PRINT, AIRBRUSH; 42 BY 78 INCHES.

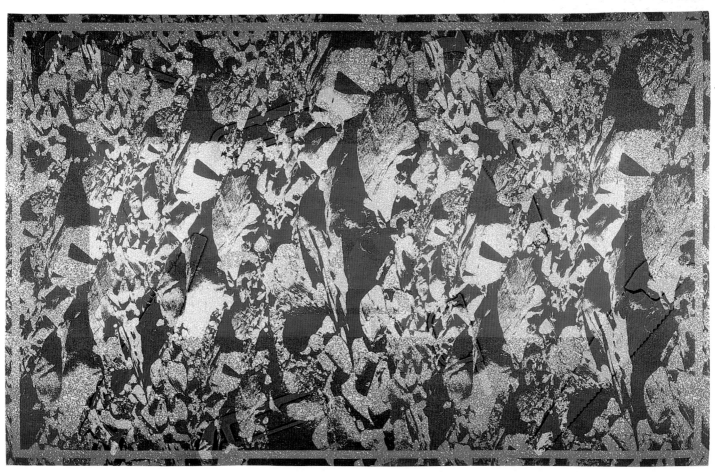

SEE SAW, 1990; LAYERED COTTON; SCREEN PRINT; 56 BY 90 INCHES. PHOTO: TOM NEFF.

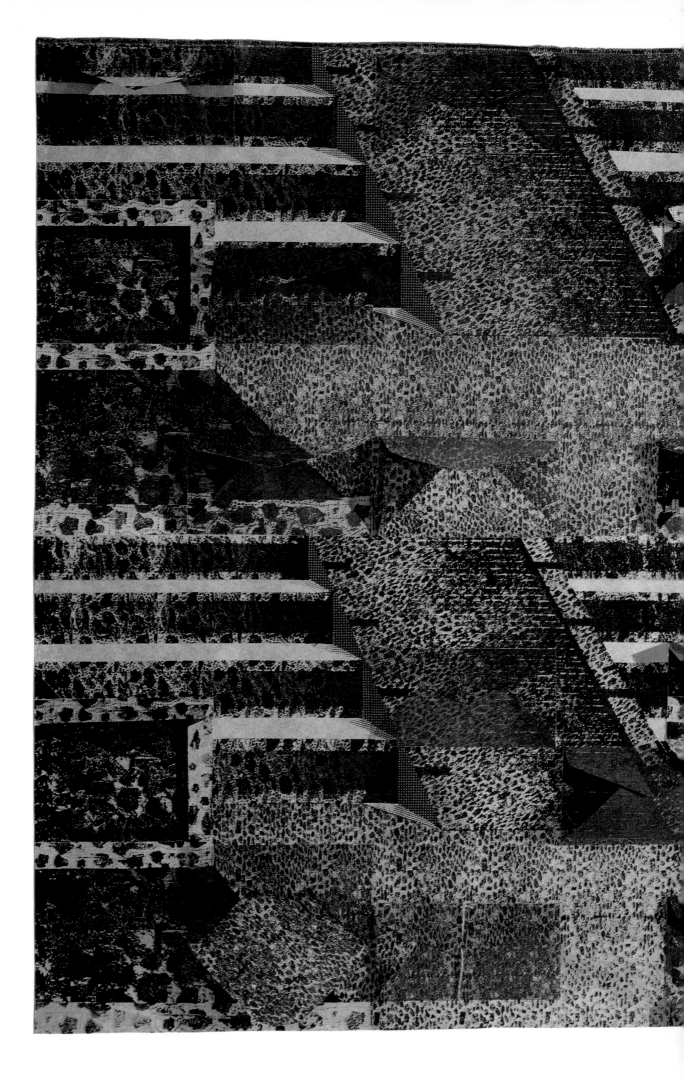

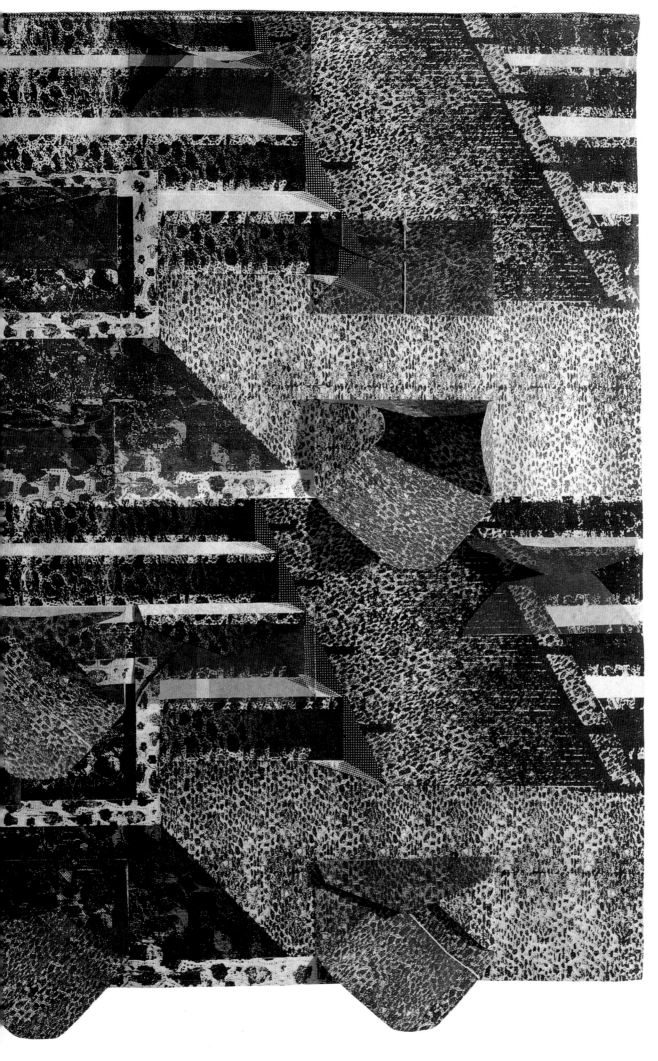

MESSAGE FROM TEOTIHUACAN, 1988; POLYESTER INTERFACING; SCREEN PRINT, PIECED; 40 BY 46 BY 3 INCHES. PHOTO: TOM NEFF.

MARNA
GOLDSTEIN
BRAUNER

On my first trip to Europe in 1970, one of the things I noticed was the same small advertising poster repeated in rows along a wall. Not only was I immediately attracted by the patterning, I was forced to look at the image over and over, making me realize the power pattern has to create a memory for the viewer. Repeat pattern is so common in daily life that it has a comforting quality.

At the time of the trip, I was just out of high school and had no notion what textile art was or that I would ever end up in it. But I am convinced that my route towards textiles began with that wall of posters. In the years since, I have been interested in doing work that plays off the comforting quality of pattern and cloth against imagery that is a bit disturbing and odd.

I began my creative life as a printmaker and photographer. I worked primarily in intaglio (etching), a process that is more sculptural than most two-dimensional processes. As I would scratch into and burnish away lines and images from copper plate, I felt that I was "building" a surface that the paper would push into, picking up the ridges of ink. This interest in the built-up surface has carried over into my work in textiles. Because cloth is so absorbent, I can soak color, marks, and images into it, then print the surface with dyes and go back to the same piece with textile pigments, glitter, and even marble dust that visually and physically sit on the surface. Beading and stitching further emphasize the layering into visual space and create a sense of physical object.

MAGNANIMOUS OPUS, 1985; LINEN, BEADS; PHOTO SILKSCREEN, DIRECT APPLICATION OF DYES, STAMPING, EMBROIDERY; 34 BY 35 INCHES. PHOTO: E. G. SCHEMPF.

Using photography allows me to capture a myriad of images from the real world and "install" these objects onto planes of cloth that are richly patterned and decorated, yet seem aged and worn. Photography has taught me that art is a subtractive process. Every image, pattern, mark, and color that I could ever want to use already exists in the world and all I do is pick and choose. I love it when a viewer assumes that I made up or altered an image, when in fact it was an object that I photographed. I have always taken an absurdist's view of the world, and I have never been disappointed. Whenever I need a particular image in my work, it appears for me to photograph.

By using photography that has a contemporary look, and playing with that imagery against pattern, surface, and format that have a deliberate historical reference, I wish to raise questions as to where each piece exists in time, and how it might function, if indeed it truly had a function.

I consider myself a storyteller, conveying narrative experiences through the juxtaposition of decorative pictorial imagery. My use of narrative and symbolic images reflects my passion for traditional textiles—everything from medieval tapestries to molas—that convey historical, religious, mythological, or social information through pictorial representation and patterning.

IN A 5000 B.C. LAYER OF A SITE IN EL FAIYAM, EGYPT, A SWATCH OF COARSE LINEN WAS FOUND IN A SMALL COOKING POT, ALONG WITH TWO FLINTS AND A FISH VERTEBRA.

When traveling in Israel and Egypt in 1983, I was particularly excited by textile objects that had obviously been intended for use in a spiritual context—the various Jewish ritual objects such as Torah covers and wrappers with their complex pictorial narratives, and the Egyptian Coptic textiles displaying ornate, seemingly bizarre, symbolic subject matter. I was intrigued not only by the decorative quality of these pieces but by their utilitarian value. Indeed, within the scope of the history of textiles, it is difficult to think of fabric outside of a practical context, even if its purpose is not immediately evident.

During a summer in Italy, I became fascinated by the small shrines and "sacred" spaces which seemed to appear around every corner. My fascination came not only from the theatricality of these spaces but also from the objects they contained—objects that glowed with the same quality of

WENT MISSING, 1987; LINEN, BEADS, SEQUINS, GLITTER; PHOTO SILKSCREEN, DIRECT APPLICATION OF DYES AND PIGMENTS; 53 BY 43 INCHES. PHOTO: MARY JO TOLE.

HORROR VACUI, 1991; LINEN; PHOTO SILKSCREEN, TIE-DYE WITH REACTIVE AND VAT DYES, PIGMENTS, STITCHED WITH WAXED LINEN; 28 BY 28-1/2 INCHES. PHOTO: RICHARD GEHRKE.

FIGLINE, 1988; LINEN, BEADS; PHOTO SILKSCREEN, DIRECT APPLICATION OF DYES AND PIGMENTS, STITCHING;
65 BY 60 INCHES. PHOTO: E. G. SCHEMPF.

unknown ritualistic intent as the Jewish and Coptic textiles. In my work,
I want to make a connection between the textile and its architectural setting, the place that has historically given cloth a profound sense of place.

While honoring the lengthy worldwide traditions of cloth making, I want
to make cloth that transcends the processes used to make it. I want my
work to convey a feeling of implied ritualistic utility and unknown mystical
association. I want to make cloth that is magical.

CAPRICCIOSA, 1988; LINEN, SILK NOIL, BEADS, SEQUINS, GLITTER; PHOTO SILKSCREEN, DIRECT
APPLICATION OF DYES AND PIGMENTS, APPLIQUE; 60 BY 45 INCHES. PHOTO: RICHARD GEHRKE.

CARCIOFI ALLA GIUDIA, 1990; LINEN, BEADS; PHOTO SILKSCREEN, DIRECT APPLICATION
OF DYES AND PIGMENTS, STITCHING; 70 BY 102 INCHES. PHOTO: RICHARD GEHRKE.

B E T S Y   S T E R L I N G
B E N J A M I N

Just north of the Imperial Palace in the textile city of Kyoto, the streets are so narrow only one small Japanese car at a time can pass. The houses are a mix of the grand and old homes of retired professors and the small, narrow homes of young families. A few feet off the street, a wooden gate opens onto a walkway through a trimmed garden to a traditional-style house in the back where I came to live in 1981. In this 70-year-old house with *tatami* (straw) floor mats, an old deep tub, and futon for sleeping, I live a life of old Japan unlike many modern Japanese in their high-rise condos.

The second-floor studio is flooded with natural light by windows on two sides affording views of distant Mt. Hiei and Shokokuji Temple. Pairs of harigi sticks for stretching silk hang on one wall, next to a selection of dyeing brushes. On top of the bookcase sit a jar of bamboo tenterhooks, a few thriving plants, and my tabby cat Mikka. The bookcase holds reference material, classical music tapes, and incense boxes. There's a stack of sketch books full of material for future paintings and kimono designs. A framed painting on silk hangs in the traditional ceremonial alcove above a stack of full-scale drawings of past work. The sliding closet doors hide multiple jars of pre-mixed acid dyes, a supply of special wax formula, and fabrics that could not be passed up on the last trip to the dye supply shop. Silk fabric is stretched across the width of the studio and my tray of dyes is placed within easy reach.

MURASAKI HAORI JACKET, 1982; SILK; KATAZOME, YUZEN, ROKETSU.

I first began doing batik in Iceland where I was throwing pots and raising babies in the early '70s. Since my interest was surface rather than form, I was advised to do my master's degree in textiles and returned to the states. Exploring the technical aspects of making photographic images on cloth and an interest in soft sculpture and wearable art were all part of my work at that time.

After a few years of teaching, I was in need of more stimulation. Over a dye pot at Arizona State University, my students encouraged me to follow my dream, and nine months later I boarded a plane for Japan with my 10-year-old daughter. In Kyoto, I happily became a student once more, for a time, and took the expected attitude of a foreigner in Japan where every visitor studies something: language, zen, tea ceremony, or other aspects of this rich culture.

After six months of *katazome* (stencil) and natural dye study and finishing my first kimono, I met master kimono artist Yusuke Tange and was accepted in his studio on a weekly basis. When I first entered his studio and noticed that there was not a chair in sight, I knew I would adapt to this new way of working or be gone within the year. As it turns out, a work table and chairs are not possible on the fragile *tatami* flooring, so I've learned to enjoy the convenience of working from a cushion.

THE CHINESE HAD A PROFOUND INFLUENCE ON BATIK MOTIFS. FROM THE NINTH CENTURY TO THE TWELFTH CENTURY, CHINA TRADED WITH JAVA FOR COLORED CLOTH. THE CHINESE BROUGHT MYTHICAL LIONS AND LYRICAL FLOWERS TO BATIK DESIGNS, ALONG WITH A NEW PALETTE OF COLORS.

It was Tange-san who taught me to design and dye kimono, to work with gold powders, and to do the wet-dye shading called *bokashi*. While proficient in a variety of techniques, his own work was done with wax resist in the *roketsu-zome* method, different from the process I had learned in Iceland. Unlike American and Indonesian batik, *roketsu* uses many blended waxes and produces no crackle. Since it is primarily brush-dyed rather than dip-dyed, shading and color control are easily possible. My style and desire for a dramatic image fit well with this technique. Years of sitting on my cushion, painting on wax heated in an electric tempura pot, adjusting the acid dyes, and playing with the *bokashi* edge have left me so confident with the process that I am able to concentrate on image.

As a child, I thought there was nothing more beautiful than the flowers in my grandmother's garden. The woods of New Hampshire, where my parents built a summer home, and dissecting flowers as well as frogs in high school biology class also made a strong impression on me. Such images filled my notebooks for years. How delighted I was when I learned that someone of the stature of Georgia O'Keeffe had been drawn to those picture-filling floral forms too, and that they were justifiable content for serious painting. Japan's textile master Kageo Miura loves to paint dancing vegetables, reconfirming my belief that subject matter need not be limited.

BLUE ALOE SCREEN, 1986; SILK; ROKETSU; 38 BY 41 INCHES. PHOTO: JAKOWSKY.

SACRED PLACES: CANYON, 1990; SILK; ROKETSU, KINSAI; 47 BY 33 INCHES. PHOTO: ITO.

THE PATH OF THE BEE, 1989; SILK; ROKETSU, KINSAI; 63 BY 36 INCHES. PHOTO: ITO.

Imagery also comes from my years in the American Southwest and from dreams and meditations. I often "sit" with an image to see it more clearly, even though a monk friend instructs that one should meditate with an empty mind. A series of sacred place paintings came from such meditations and were further developed during trips to Europe, the United States, Southeast Asia, and Australia. The Japanese sensitivity to color has encouraged me to look carefully and to redefine my palette. The hot primaries of Arizona have been greatly softened by the traditional colors of Kyoto, filtered through rain, cloud, and haze. My sense of color took another jump recently after spending time in Australia where the vivid blue of the sky and red of the land is unequalled.

Joseph Campbell once said that "a real artist is the one who has learned to recognize and to render. . .the 'radiance' of all things as an epiphany or [a] showing forth of the truth." My desire to look closely at objects has resulted in an aspect in my painting where perspective is lost and the foreground overwhelms the background. Giant orchids float above Arizona mountains; peony stamens wrap around rocky crags, looking for a new vision, a true essence, a radiance within. Where better to seek this recognition than in Kyoto.

FOR GEORGIA, 1986; SILK; ROKETSU; 66 BY 37 INCHES. PHOTO: JAKOWSKY.

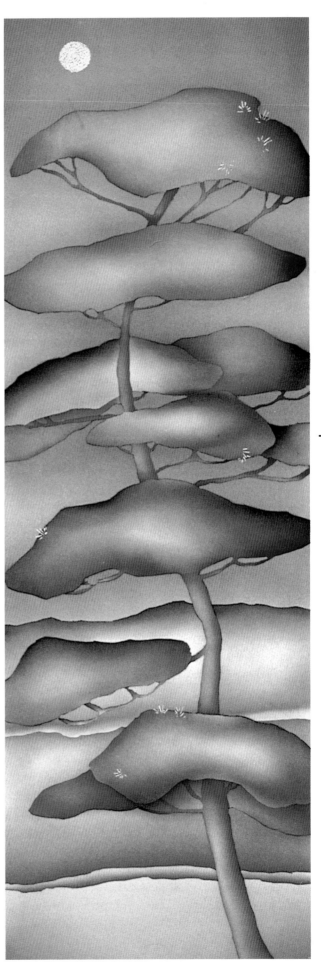

GAIA SUITE: PALM, 1992; SILK; ROKETSU, KINSAI;
15 BY 38 INCHES. PHOTO: T. SUZUKI.

SETTING SUN, 1991; SILK; ROKETSU;
16 BY 47 INCHES. PHOTO: T. SUZUKI.

J A S O N
P O L L E N

The activity of building images out of brush strokes, collaged fabric fragments, overlays of luminous fiber reactive dyes on thirsty silk satin reconnects me with the timeless, wordless world of the solitary child.

I remember ecstatic summers on Fire Island, New York where I spent most of my days letting moist, warm sand slip through my fingers. I watched as first a mound, then a wizard's castle would emerge at that magical crossroads where the sea and the shore join hands. Then and there it was seaweed and shells and twigs which were arranged by determined fingers, eager to record revelations of the mind's journey. Passing waves taught me lessons on impermanence and constancy.

A one-way ticket to Paris in the early 1960s landed me in Montmartre, where I peddled paintings in the shadows of Picasso and Modigliani. After nearly four years of wondering where the next meal would come from, I received a phone call that changed the course and direction of my path. Jack Prince, veteran New York based textile designer, called to ask if I would show his portfolio to the French fashion designers. I did. The success of his collection led me to attempt my own, at first crude, textile designs. Eventually, I uncovered the vast worldwide textiles industry and its eternal need for new images. Regular freelance work designing sheets, or bathing suits, or scarves, provided me the freedom to explore fabric and dye, and to evolve from a painter on canvas to a painter on silk. Two years in India brought me closest to the source of our textile heritage.

FREESIA, 1983; SILK, FIBER REACTIVE DYES; SILKSCREEN, OFFSET AND BLOCK PRINTING, DIRECT PAINTING, DISCHARGE DYEING; 54 BY 108 INCHES.

EARLIEST EVIDENCE FOR AWARENESS OF THE SILKWORM IS IN THE FORM OF AN ARTIFICIALLY CUT COCOON DISCOVERED IN THE NEOLITHIC AGE LAYERS OF HSI-YIN-TS'UN, SHANSI PROVINCE, CHINA. THE SPECIES BOMBYX MORI PROVIDED THE KEY TO HIGH QUALITY SILK SINCE IT CAN BE UNWOUND IN AN UNBROKEN, CONTINUOUS STRAND.

Returning to the United States in 1976, I learned that I had the credentials, the motivation, and the expertise required of the teaching profession. After five years at Parsons School of Design and Pratt Institute, I came to the Kansas City Art Institute. The road ahead points to an increasing connection to the students, to the as-yet-unexplored layers beneath the surface of silk, and, of course, to digging ever deeper into the nature of being and becoming.

TERRA EPHEMERA, 1991; SILK, FIBER REACTIVE DYES; SILKSCREEN, OFFSET AND BLOCK PRINTING, DIRECT PAINTING, DISCHARGE DYEING;
27 BY 49 INCHES. PHOTO: LUKE JORDAN.

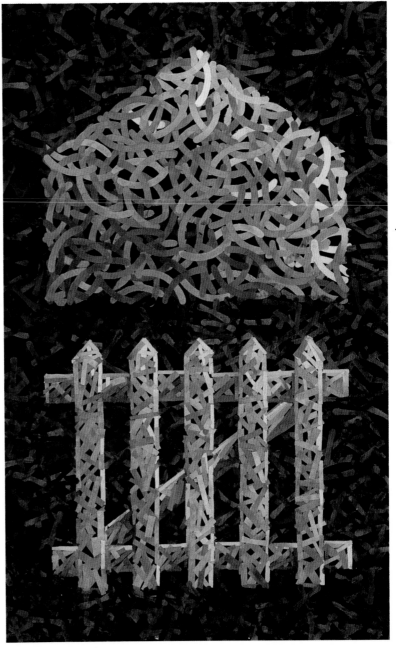

UNTITLED, 1991; SILK, FIBER REACTIVE DYES; SILKSCREEN, OFFSET AND BLOCK
PRINTING, DIRECT PAINTING, DISCHARGE DYEING; 20 BY 30 INCHES.
PHOTO: E. G. SCHEMPF.

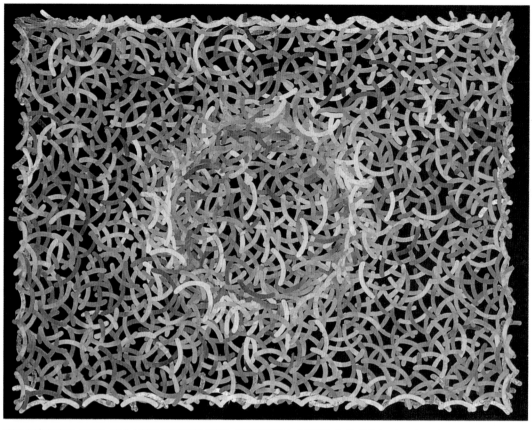

SOLAR WIND, 1991; SILK, FIBER REACTIVE DYES; SILKSCREEN, OFFSET AND BLOCK PRINTING, DIRECT PAINTING, DISCHARGE DYEING; 20 BY 30 INCHES. PHOTO: E. G. SCHEMPF.

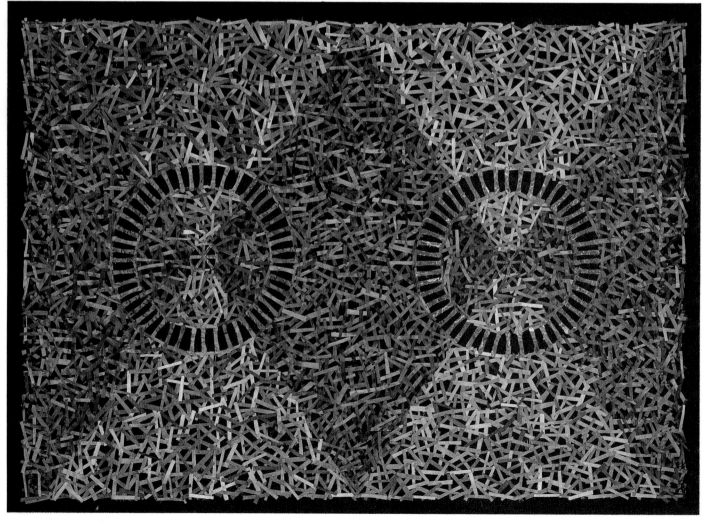

TWO, #1, 1991; SILK, FIBER REACTIVE DYES; SILKSCREEN, OFFSET AND BLOCK PRINTING, DIRECT PAINTING, DISCHARGE DYEING; 20 BY 30 INCHES. PHOTO: E. G. SCHEMPF.

TRINITY, 1990; SILK, FIBER REACTIVE DYES; SILKSCREEN, OFFSET AND BLOCK PRINTING, DIRECT PAINTING, DISCHARGE DYEING; 18 BY 43 INCHES. PHOTO: E. G. SCHEMPF.

13 BANDS, 1992; SILK, FIBER REACTIVE DYES; SILKSCREEN, OFFSET AND BLOCK PRINTING, DIRECT PAINTING, DISCHARGE DYEING; 40 BY 60 INCHES. PHOTO: GARY SUTTON.

A N A   L I S A
H E D S T R O M

When designing, I usually have a mental sketch or direction, but I like to keep the process and decision making very open-ended. I pin fabric on the wall or a mannequin, leave it for days, add a piece, turn the fabric ninety degrees, cut, and rearrange. This way the fabric talks to me. My clothing is essentially collaged, combining colors and piecing pattern against pattern. I think of this process as composing. Rhythm, scale, harmony, dissonance, mood: these are terms that are used by both visual artists and musicians, and I do like the idea that my clothes could be "musical." Originally I made pleated wall pieces but found that the body offered a better sculptural opportunity. There seems to be an intense visceral appeal for pleated cloth. Certainly, in clothing, it adds sensuous and sensual dimensions. Resist pleated forms, as resist dyed patterns, allude to nature: shells, feathers, reptile skin, mushroom gills. Ancient atavistic associations? I sometimes think so.

Certain themes run through my work and may resurface at any time in a new way. My designs often have a visual reference to clouds and sky. Partially, this is the intrinsic nature of the arashi shibori dyeing technique. Arashi means "storm," and this traditional Japanese technique creates patterns resembling rain, water, and wind.

Color is paramount. My color sense is acidic rather than sweet, opaque and saturated rather than transparent or pastel. Turquoise, for my

sensibility, is a boring color unless it is adjacent to unexpected colors such as ochre, rust, plum, olive. Then it sings. Shaded colors have held a strong attraction for me since I began working in 1975. I sometimes think the appeal of graduated color relates to the timelessness of the horizon at sunset or sunrise. I can't stop using shaded yellow squares. I was captured by some charming shaded pink and yellow sugar candies; ideas come from everywhere.

Because I often work with folded and precisely pleated fabric, geometric designs became another natural direction. I like to challenge myself and to stretch the apparent limits of technique. For example, creating both large and small geometric shapes on the same piece of wrapped fabric or retaining pleats by "capturing" the process of shibori. No one else might be as satisfied by a technical tour de force. I work on the faith that if my mind and senses are pleasantly involved in the process, so will the viewer be pleasurably engaged.

Shibori, particularly arashi shibori, is the source of my work. My designs and approach have diverged greatly from the Japanese tradition, and

THE EARLIEST FIND OF COMPLETE CLOTHING IN GREECE WAS AN ANKLE LENGTH ROBE IN A SITE DATED AT 1000 B.C. IT WAS MADE OF TWO PIECES OF CLOTH SEWN UP THE SIDES, AND WAS FOLDED CAREFULLY INSIDE A BRONZE JAR.

I describe the process as simply resist dyed, unless I am using strictly traditional shibori patterns. I have also worked extensively since 1978 with smocking machines to produce stitch resist as well as shirred and embellished textiles. I use silk acid dyes, fiber reactive dyes, vat dyes, textile paints and pigments, and discharge agents. I immerse, paint, spray, and dip. Dyes are an important part of my work, but it is not the dye itself, but knowing the dye that makes for particular results. A very observant eye (all my best results came from developing mistakes and accidents) and lots of exploring make the difference. A test sample should never be just a success or a failure, but information for the next piece.

Designing clothes is essentially a collaborative process: models, stylists, photographers, and store buyers might all have their input, but finally the wearer completes the garment. More than anything, I like the quiet time in my studio; but I also like the idea that my clothes leave with a mysterious future of their own to be found, enjoyed, and shared.

TUNIC AND SKIRT, 1987; CREPE DE CHINE; HAND DYED, PLEATED. PHOTO: CRAIG MOREY.

WOOL KNIT, 1988, COLLABORATION WITH JANET LIPKIN (MACHINE KNITTING) AND K. LEE MANUEL (BELT); POLE WRAP RESIST DYED, DISCHARGED. PHOTO: BARRY SHAPIRO.

DRESS AND SCARVES, 1992; ORGANZA,
CREPE DE CHINE; STITCH RESIST DYED.
PHOTO: BARRY SHAPIRO.

NIGHT SKY JACKET II, 1989; ONISHIBO CREPE;
POLE WRAP RESIST DYED, PIECED.
PHOTO: BARRY SHAPIRO.

 E R M A   M A R T I N
Y O S T

My life as an artist began as an abstract landscape painter in the late 1960s. Since that time my work has gone through several transitions, but certain things have remained constant: I retain a compulsion for surface quality and texture; the forces, cycles, and dramas of nature intrigue me and serve thematically in my work.

Nature presents us with things so much larger than life, but which can still serve as metaphors for life. This fact became particularly vivid to me in 1976 as my photographer husband Leon and I traveled throughout the Southwestern United States. The colors in my palette changed when I returned to the studio. The blues and greens of my environs were replaced by reds and ochres. We have made numerous return trips and that vast, colorful landscape has become an integral part of my being.

The women in my family were Mennonite quilters. Sewing was a great interest in my youth, from hand stitching doll clothes to working in a sewing factory summers between college years. Even though I never helped make a quilt, throughout my childhood I watched the process from beginning to end many times. I enjoyed the traditional geometric patterns and could be quite opinionated about the arrangement of the quilt blocks, even then.

During a time out from painting, I made some quilted jackets, never thinking of them as having a connection to my art work. But as I get older, I
am learning that all things do connect and I make less distinction between
the activities of daily life and art. Commenting on my sewing efforts, a
friend remarked that I ought to exhibit the jackets. I didn't want to do
that, but I did start to think about how I might incorporate fabric into my
work. What evolved were two series which I describe as quilt/painting
combines. Here, a pieced traditional quilt top and a painting are hinged
together and framed as one unit. The connection is mainly one of design
and color. I continued this work into the early 1980s when I took a winter
off to do some preliminary sketches for an upcoming show.

That was not the typical way I approach my work, but I wanted to work in
a new direction. I had a shoe box full of Polaroid photos I had taken on
our trips to the Southwest. It had become Leon's passion to document
the art left on canyon walls over a thousand years ago by the Anasazi
Indians. Many of the images are in remote places, so it became my job to
take the Polaroid shots, which got labeled on site. I had hoped some day
to use these photos as a resource.

A NUMBER OF
CLOTHS WERE
FOUND IN A
SIXTH-CENTURY
B.C. DIG IN
GERMANY:
SILKS, WOOLS,
LINENS IN
A VARIETY OF
TECHNIQUES,
DYED AND
UNDYED.
THE ARTISANS
DID NOT
HESITATE
TO STACK
TECHNIQUES
ONTO A
SINGLE CLOTH.

As I sketched, I found that I was planning pieces I didn't know how to make using my current techniques. I especially wanted to incorporate dramatic skies. A friend suggested I try the cyanotype process. I spent the entire summer in the darkroom, armed with Bea Nettles' book, **Breaking the Rules**. As I experimented that summer, I came up with a way to draw the rock art images that seemed compatible with my work. I finally had found an expression that felt authentic and my own, not one influenced by former teachers or the work of other artists.

So as to have a broader color palette and not be limited by the blue and white of the cyanotype process, I eventually taught myself other photo processes. Essentially I was creating my own fabrics through these photographic images on cloth. I became less interested in commercial fabrics and began to paint again, but this time on lightweight duck, which could be cut up like yardage. Along the way I added machine embroidery, beads, bones, and feathers. In the end, I had a layered sandwich of fabric in a reinterpretation of the quilt.

My current interests focus on the environment and ecology. Initially I had hoped to protest issues such as ancient forests being cut down, paper being produced and not recycled, and the amount of lumber that is exported. As the work evolved, though, it turned into more of a celebration of trees and a pristine environment. I am letting the work take its own direction.

HERD LISTENING, 1988; COTTON, BLENDED FABRIC, VELVET, PAPER, FABRIC PAINT, COLORED PENCIL; MACHINE PIECED AND QUILTED, CYANOTYPE; 23 BY 27 INCHES.

CALLING THE RAINS, 1990; COTTON DUCK, CHEESE CLOTH, BEADS, FABRIC PAINT, PASTELS; MACHINE PIECED AND QUILTED, MACHINE EMBROIDERY, CYANOTYPE, HEAT TRANSFER; 34 BY 30 INCHES.

CALLING THE RAINS, DETAIL.

I follow a maxim attributed to Jasper Johns: "Do something, do something to that, and then do something to that." In other words, don't sit around waiting for inspiration, for it seldom comes in a blinding flash; it comes from the "do"ing. As the meaning or expression takes form and becomes a little clearer, I proceed. At some point, the process takes over and informs and directs me. Eventually the piece tells me it is complete.

PLACE OF VISIONS, 1990; COTTON DUCK, HANDMADE PAPER, METALLIC THREAD, COLORED PENCIL; MACHINE PIECED AND QUILTED, CYANOTYPE, KWIK-PRINT; 40 BY 34 INCHES.

PLACE IN THE PINES, 1992; COTTON, METALLIC AND IRIDESCENT FABRIC, FABRIC SCRAPS, FABRIC PAINT, PASTELS; MACHINE PIECED, QUILTED AND EMBROIDERED, HEAT TRANSFER, CYANOTYPE; 24 BY 32 INCHES.

NEW DAWN, DETAIL.

NEW DAWN, 1991; COTTON DUCK,
METALLIC AND RAYON THREAD;
MACHINE PIECED AND EMBROI-
DERED, CYANOTYPE, KWIK-PRINT;
17 BY 14 INCHES.

A N N E M C K E N Z I E
N I C K O L S O N

Perspective is an interest I've explored since I began working with fiber. I want to create the illusion of three-dimensional space.

To attain this illusion in my early pieces, I set up spatial situations by making tiny embroidery stitches in varying shades and densities—this took many painstaking hours. I switched to the airbrush to create subtler or more vibrant color and hard or soft edges. While I lost the texture and "hand" of the seed stitching, the work is more spontaneous and I can make more pieces.

I use household items like masking tape, contact paper, or freezer paper to make stencils and I experiment on pattern with the airbrush. Then I think about how to incorporate embroidery into the piece. Currently I use machine embroidery and do not even attempt to mimic hand embroidery since the purpose is different. Embroidery is the line in my work, and I draw with it to define, distort, or emphasize. Marbling is also used to create a smoky, indefinite, and, I think, beautiful background.

In my recent figurative work, I often piece fabrics together, then apply a stencil, and then airbrush. This creates a complex illusion of transparent layers on which the machine embroidered figure plays hide-and-seek. Sharp, clear geometric shapes are then appliqued on top, trapping the figure in the space behind.

ZIG ZAG IX, 1980; COTTON, RICKRACK; HAND SEWN, AIRBRUSHED WITH FIBER REACTIVE DYE, EMBROIDERY; 6-1/2 BY 9-1/2 INCHES.

Certain guidelines are kept in mind as I work. I try to use each technique to best advantage—to develop the characteristics that are unique to that technique. I use airbrush to create repeat patterns. Though this is similar to what could be done with silkscreen, the use of airbrush creates subtle color changes that begin in one corner and end in another, no matter what the pattern does. By contrasting these soft edges with sharp, clear embroidered edges, atmospheric perspective begins to happen—some lines are in focus and seem close, others are out of focus and recede. Repeat patterns are an exciting visual structure for me.

A comfortable command of technique allows me to focus on imagery as well as the general feeling I want my pieces to convey: that there is a field of energy where something is happening. Repeat patterns provide a rhythm which gives me something to respond to. The working process becomes a dialogue between me and what is already happening on the fabric.

Though the making of textile artworks often involves intensive hours of discipline, there are many phases of play and satisfaction, and both a sensual and intellectual enjoyment of the materials and processes.

FROM MIDDLE MINOAN TIMES, 1800-1600 B.C., WE SEE A SORT OF PLAYFULNESS WITH DESIGN ELEMENTS. OPTICAL ILLUSION AND A TENDENCY TO PLAY WITH SPACE, TO MAKE FIGURE OF GROUND AND GROUND OF FIGURE, ARE TYPICAL OF THE TEXTILES OF THESE ANCIENT PEOPLE OF CRETE.

FRACTURED, 1989; COTTON POPLIN; STENCIL, FIBER REACTIVE DYE, AIRBRUSHED WITH FIBER PAINTS, EMBROIDERY; 28-3/8 BY 25-7/8 INCHES.
PHOTO: PIERSON PHOTOGRAPHICS.

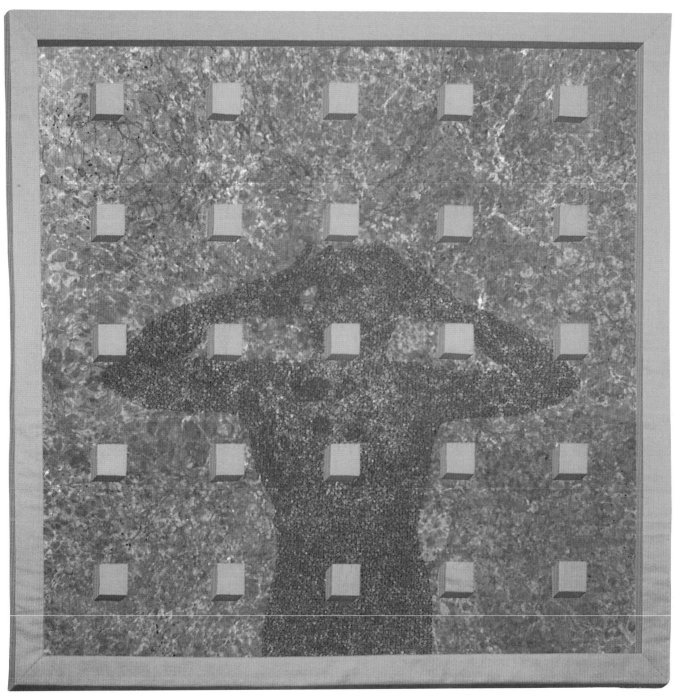

WHAT'S OUT THERE?, 1992; COTTON; MARBLED WITH CARRAGEEN AND PIGMENTED DRAWING INKS, APPLIQUE, MACHINE
EMBROIDERY, PIECING; 40 BY 40 INCHES.

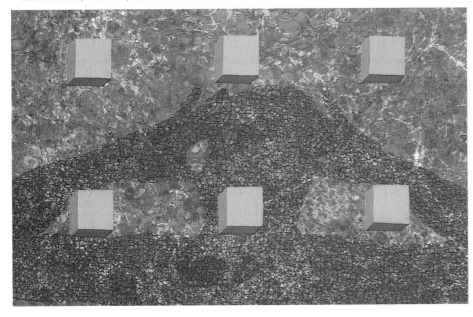

WHAT'S OUT THERE?, DETAIL.

AURORA BOREALIS, 1990; COTTON; STENCIL, FIBER REACTIVE DYE, AIRBRUSHED WITH REGULAR, IRIDESCENT, AND PEARLESCENT FIBER PAINTS, EMBROIDERY; 43 BY 49 INCHES.

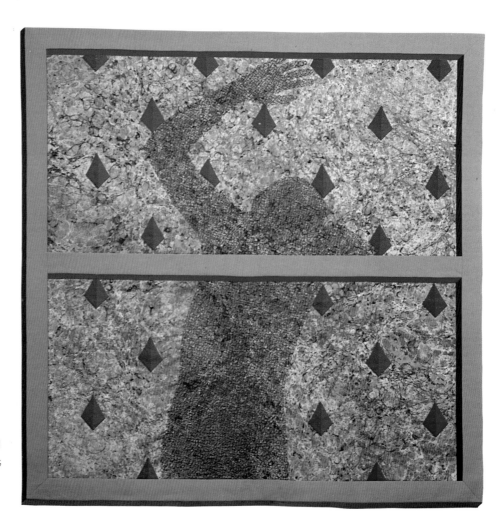

TOO HOT, 1992; COTTON; MARBLED WITH CARRAGEEN AND PIGMENTED DRAWING INKS, APPLIQUE, MACHINE EMBROIDERY, PIECING; 40 BY 40 INCHES.

TIGER CLOTH, 1990; COTTON POPLIN; STENCIL, AIRBRUSHED WITH FIBER PAINT, EMBROIDERY; 40-1/4 BY 33-1/4 INCHES.

M I C H A E L
O L S Z E W S K I

My work chronicles and recreates the essence of feeling and emotions that have occurred between aspects of myself, other people, and varying circumstances. I use line, symbolic forms, colors, and textures to convey personal issues of aging, separation, and life's passing. It is through this iconography that I attempt a greater understanding of the issues that life presents.

The emotional participation in the aging process of my parents, the death of my father, and the loss of friends to AIDS have had a profound effect on images I have created in my work. Although the forms I use are deceptively simple geometric shapes, they are laden with emotional meaning for me. The complexity of meaning arises from their placement, juxtaposition, and tension. The visual context is reinforced by color, pattern, and texture. In some of the pieces, I have used transparent silk over a background of fabric that has been dyed, pleated, appliqued, and embroidered. This transparent veil represents layers of awareness and levels of understanding which continue to evolve through intense personal introspection.

The issues that I am compelled to deal with arise from within my being and are not about life's lighter matters. For many years, I struggled with personal identity, feeling different and alienated, searching for a self-realization that would allow me to be more accepting of whom I am. Often my work is seen as somber and emotionally serious. This is exactly what I intend. From childhood through college, art was a way

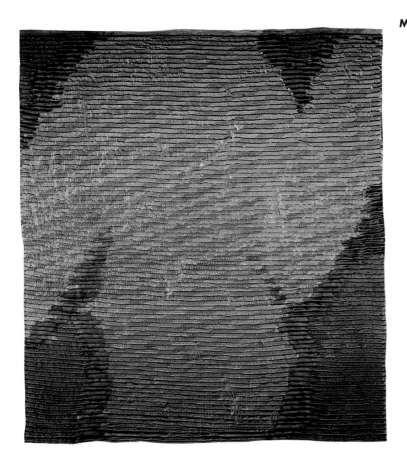

for me to express visual beauty while masking internal turmoil.

While in graduate school at Cranbrook Academy of Art, I experienced a turning point in my artistic development. The environment at Cranbrook, either real or as perceived by me, allowed me to look more closely at myself and express these discoveries in a forum that was amenable to different artistic points of view. I learned that one's work could be the vehicle for personal expression whatever that source may be. After this discovery, it was easier to assess my thoughts and feelings and understand my emotions. There is always a struggle to merge the issues of the heart and mind in order to create an image that will be evocative and yet communicate in an articulate and powerful voice.

In my fabric pieces, I incorporate traditional batik processes and Japanese shibori dyeing techniques with hand stitching. I use stitching and embroidery to create linear markings which are reminiscent of handwriting and drawing. Pieced and appliqued fabrics are used, echoing and continuing the history of quiltmaking where cloth becomes the documentation for people's lives. I also research work with which I feel a spiritual and artistic kinship. The pre-Columbian textiles of the Nazca Indians, the painting of the Russian Constructivists, works of Sonia Delauney, Marsden Hartley, and Mark Rothko, and the creative language of the abstract expressionists are inspiring to me for their directness and precise, powerful use of color and form.

AT THE HOHMICHELE, GERMANY DIG, 900-600 B.C., A TEXTILE WAS UNEARTHED IN WHICH SILK WAS BOTH WOVEN INTO THE GARMENT AND EMBROIDERED INTO IT, DONE WITH OVERCAST AND STEM STITCHES.

MOURNING, 1989; NEW AND ANTIQUE SILKS; WAX RESIST, ARASHI SHIBORI, HAND PAINTED DYES, HAND STITCHING, APPLIQUE; 20-1/2 BY 28-1/4 INCHES.

MY PARENTS, 1988; NEW AND ANTIQUE SILKS; WAX RESIST AND HAND PAINTED DYES, APPLIQUE;
19 BY 18 INCHES.

STORM, 1987; SILK HABUTAI; WAX RESIST AND HAND PAINTED DYES, EMBROIDERY; 16 BY 15 INCHES.

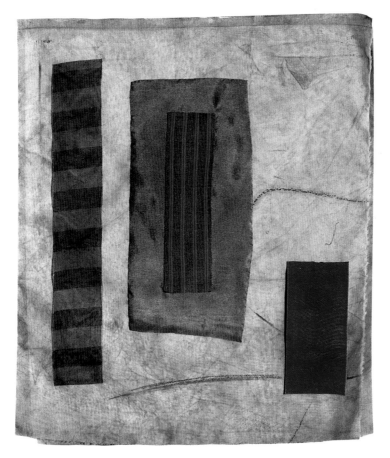

IN PASSING #1, 1992; SILK, NYLON; WAX RESIST, HAND PAINTED DYES, DRAWING, APPLIQUE, EMBROIDERY; 15-1/2 BY 12-1/2 INCHES.

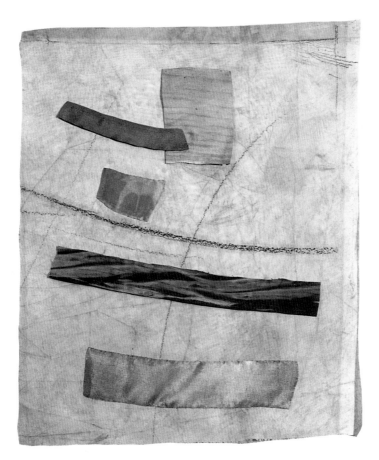

IN PASSING #2, 1992; SILK, NYLON; WAX RESIST, HAND PAINTED DYES, DRAWING, APPLIQUE, EMBROIDERY; 15-1/2 BY 12-1/2 INCHES.

SORROW, 1990; SILK HABUTAI; WAX RESIST, ARASHI SHIBORI, HAND PAINTED DYES, APPLIQUE, EMBROIDERY; 35 BY 32 INCHES.

D ' A R C I E
B E Y T E B I E R E

One of my most vivid memories is when my parents bought me an easel
at the age of ten, and I would stand and draw along with Jon Gnagy on
the TV set. As an undergraduate college student, I worked in clay sculpture, being mainly interested in form and the surface texture of the clay.
Towards the end of my senior year, a performance artist visiting the college
wore a costume covered in soft-sculpture hands. It really made an impression on me, and I did a sculpture series combining clay and fabric.

After graduating, I became an artist-in-residence, traveling around
Washington State teaching art to kindergarten through college-age students. All the while I was teaching, I was also doing studio work, focusing
on soft sculpture and batik. Fabric was a medium which really worked well
with my traveling lifestyle. I could take pieces or parts of pieces with me
wherever I went and work on some aspect of the piece almost anywhere.

One evening I went to an open house at an art school where there was a
demonstration on shibori techniques. I was taken by the high contrast,
intricate patterns, and texture of the indigo-and-white cloth. Something
clicked. This was the medium that I had been looking for. I asked the
woman in charge of the demonstration where I could learn more about
this process. She told me that her teacher would be back in two years
and I could probably take her workshop then. I said I wanted to go
home and do this now. She copied her notes for me.

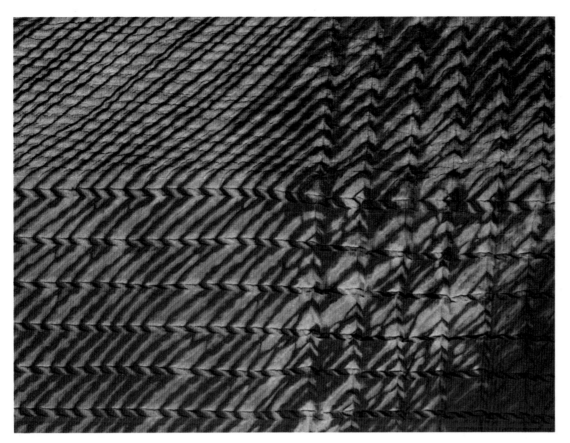

WALL PIECE, DETAIL, 1985; SILK BROADCLOTH, VAT AND DIRECT DYES; HAND PLEATING, ARASHI SHIBORI.

I made samples of traditional techniques; I taught myself about dyes by experimenting and asking questions of local suppliers. After about a year and a half, I decided to go to graduate school in order to have concentrated studio time to really explore shibori. I became more masterful of the processes and could work on ideas instead of technique.

One ongoing series that started then is my shawl series. I treat the fabric like a painter's canvas. I can work with color, line, and patterning without having to worry about whether it will fit someone; I can be as experimental as I want. This format allows me to push ideas and to try new combinations of techniques. It gives me total freedom in creating.

Over the years I've realized that, when the texture is left in as part of the design effect, shibori makes for a very fragile cloth. On the one hand, this is okay. The fabric is treated with the same care as an antique wedding dress or heirloom jewelry, with a sense of preciousness. On the other hand, I want my fabric to be somewhat predictable, to look the same five years from now, even if it has been worn many times. And then again, maybe a piece of art that would change with use and time is kind of an interesting thought.

Thinking about the fragility of the pleating texture led me to experiment with more permanent ways in which the cloth could be manipulated.

HAVING
MIRACULOUSLY
SURVIVED
THE MILLENNIA,
THE OLDEST
COMPLETE
EGYPTIAN
GARMENT
EXTANT IS A
FRINGED AND
PLEATED SHIRT
FROM TARKHAN,
CA. 3000 B.C.

I tried hand smocking, reed pleater smocking leaving the threads in the fabric, a variety of iron-on interfacings, and leaving the actual shibori process thread in the fabric when appropriate. This leaving of the process threads in my work has become a signature of my pieces.

Wanting permanency of texture in my work has led me on a new adventure of learning to spin and weave. I became aware of a type of fabric called collapse weave cloth a few years back. The fabric has a permanent sort of wild, undulating texture. The warp and/or weft threads of the fabric are initially overspun so that, when woven, they will twist back on themselves, creating a rippling cloth. This process insures a permanently textured cloth of sorts, no matter what surface treatment is inflicted upon it. An already textured cloth combined with a shibori-textured surface seems to be the perfect solution.

Like most fiber artists, I have saved scraps and sample pieces for many years. Using this fabric as inspiration, I am producing a number of quilts—my "Scrapbook Series." I'm not in the habit of keeping a written journal, but I know where every piece of fabric in these quilts came from, and I'm reminded of all sorts of past adventures. This series is my journal in cloth.

FOOTHILLS, 1987; SILK BROADCLOTH, FIBER REACTIVE AND VAT DYES; ARASHI SHIBORI; 22 BY 54 INCHES.

SHIBORI SHAWL, DETAIL, 1988; SILK TWILL, FIBER REACTIVE DYE; HAND PLEATING, ARASHI SHIBORI.

SHAWL AND RED DRESS, 1989; SILK, RAYON, VELVET; HAND SMOCKING, ARASHI SHIBORI; SHAWL, 90 BY 30 INCHES.

SHIBORI QUILT, NO. 1, 1992; SILK, RAYON, COTTON, BEADS, DYE; ARASHI SHIBORI, STITCH SHIBORI, KUMO SHIBORI; 72 BY 68 INCHES.

ANNE
LINDBERG

In *The Sense of Sight*, British writer John Berger said, "To approach experience. . .is not like approaching a house. Experience is indivisible and continuous, at least within a single lifetime and perhaps over many lifetimes.
I never have the impression that my experience is entirely my own, and it
often seems to me that it preceded me. In any case, experience folds upon
itself, refers backwards and forwards to itself through the referents of hope
and fear, and by the use of metaphor, which is at the origin of language, it
is continually comparing like with unlike, what is small with what is large,
what is near with what is distant. And so the act of approaching a given
moment of experience involves both scrutiny (closeness) and the capacity
of connect (distance)."

At its core, my work acknowledges the layered and cyclical nature of
experience, emotion, and time. It is from nature's subtle rhythms and
intonations that I find the initial impetus to make textiles and drawings.
I continually try to embody in my work the power and vulnerability of
nature's mysteries.

In the pliable plane of cloth, I am working to find visual and physical
equivalents that mirror the sensations of time, place, and sound. Just as
memory and sensation are always in the process of change, unrestrained by
forces of nature, the images are never locked in place. Ideas about light
often serve as catalysts—putting other senses in motion—sound, color,

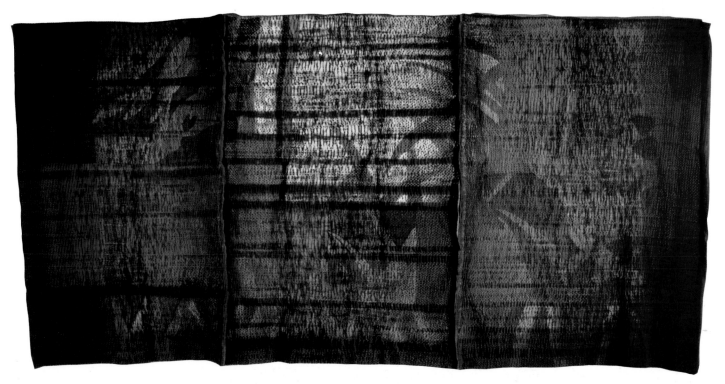

GATHERING TWILIGHT BLUE ON FRIDA'S GARDEN PATH, 1988; COTTON, INDIGO; GATHERED, STITCHED, DYED; 7 BY 14 FEET.

space, temperature. I want the images, shapes, and colors to have the mysterious quality of objects only half-materialized, on the verge of dissolution or concretion. The image seems to come from within the cloth, or behind it, as if there is something back there to bring to the surface. I often think of the cloth as a skin which holds meaning and air. The cloth is a clearing, a place to come into.

Simply by its direct associations to sky and to sea, the symbolic and emotional meanings of the color blue stand between, and so present questions to me. The long and deeply embedded mythologies and traditions of dyeing with indigo are strong, unspoken sources for all of my work. I think about indigo blue, and find myself continually using it for many reasons—ethnographic, historical, formal, conceptual, and purely visceral. It is a complex, dense, compelling color that I can see is always changing. Yet, it is the power of indigo to connect and to be almost fundamental which is its essence.

I use cloth because of its substance, intimacy, and tactility. The chosen and accumulated materials of this work—discarded cottons, silks, and linens, collage fabrics, threads of all kinds, sticks, paint, wire, indigo, graphite— become substances in hand which I move, change, pattern, tend, question, cut, and posit. The activity of making I see as analogous to thoughts about the intricacy of experience. A stitch can connote a moving thought,

INDIGO BLUE
FIBER CAUGHT
UP IN A BONE
IMPLEMENT WAS
DISCOVERED AT
THE CAVE SITE IN
LATE NEOLITHIC
(3000-2500
B.C.)
ADAOUSTE,
FRANCE.

and a haze of color or pattern can symbolize a time of day. New work investigates the accumulation and positioning of many similar repetitive elements as building blocks in the surface, image, and structure of the textile. The sheer physicality which results from action and surface manipulation encourages perception of the work to be, all at once, visual and sensory.

Making is yielding, quietly bringing to bear an understanding which connects me with the rhythms of life. Metaphorically, the cycles of time and experience thought about in this work evolve with each breath. It is with words and silences, motion and rest, that I keep working.

WELLING, 1992; ACRYLIC, GRAPHITE, GOUACHE, NYLON THREAD ON PAPER; 19 BY 18 INCHES.

SO MANY SOUNDS AT NIGHT I, 1989; COTTON, INDIGO; PIECED, STITCHED, GATHERED, COLLAGE; 46 BY 48 INCHES.

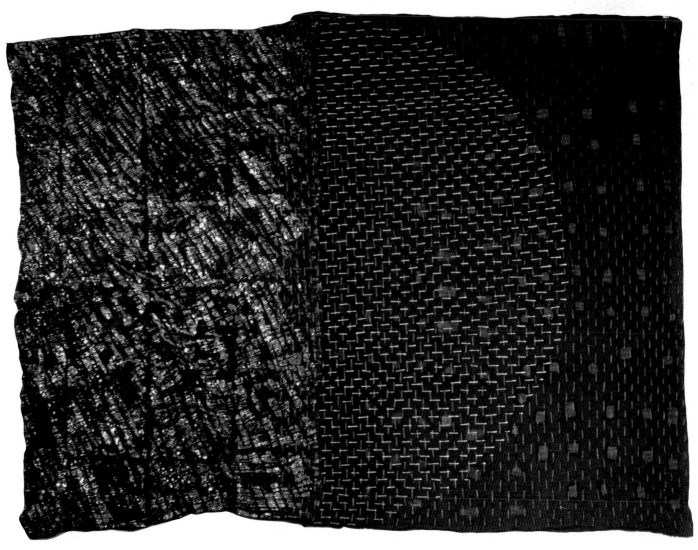

MOON AND WORDS, 1990; COTTON, INDIGO, GOLD LEAF; DYED, STITCHED, GATHERED, PIECED, PLEATED, COLLAGE; 28 BY 38 INCHES.

K A T H E R I N E
W E S T P H A L

While it seems I have been printing textiles forever, the commitment became total in the 1950s.

I think back to my first experiences as a child, of making visual statements: the magic of the mark of a crayon, of filling a brush with color and letting it flow over a surface, or of cutting and pasting. These acts became a life-long passion. I prefer doing this to anything else—not only the techniques, but the entire thought process.

I want to become a link in that long chain of human activity, the patterning of cloth on any surface available. I have learned from many cultures and pay homage to them. My work is pretty much autobiographical and narrative. It records my travel, anything I see or experience can pop out in my work, the connection being most often intuitive. I draw constantly in museums and, because life is so speeded up, I record with a camera as well as a sketch book.

In the 1970s, while teaching at the University of California at Davis, I experimented with the office copying machine and later the color machine. I was not content to just reproduce an image, but used the copier as a drawing tool, hand manipulating the image as the machine scanned it. These images were then printed on heat transfer paper, allowing me to incorporate drawings, photographs, and words into my work.

BEETLE WINGS, 1968, DETAIL; COTTON VELVETEEN; PASTE RESIST, VAT DYED; FULL PIECE 46 BY 34 INCHES.

This gives my storytelling a layered or spatial look and connects ideas and clarifies the visual message.

Today, I own a Sharp 5000 color copier. It lives in the corner of my studio. I use it constantly to produce images to be heat transported onto fabric, paper, or bark. Other dyeing, printing, and painting methods are mixed into the object. I cut and paste, patch and embroider, and fringe. I make garments wearable, or for the wall, or I cover gourds with images printed on thin Japanese rice paper. I make things constantly.

There is not enough time in the day to work. There is not enough room to store that work. My husband and I are constantly expanding our work space, and our dogs Sam and Molly have learned to live with it. They too are part of the art of doing and living.

A LARGE CLOTH DECORATED WITH MYTHOLOGICAL FIGURES WAS FOUND IN A FOURTH-CENTURY B.C. TOMB IN UKRAINE. THE PERSONAGES INCLUDE ATHENA, NIKE, PHAIDRA, AND JOCASTA.

BILL GRAHAM, 1992, DETAIL; BARK CLOTH; PHOTOCOPY, HEAT TRANSFER; FULL PIECE 48 BY 44 INCHES.

HAWAIIAN KITSCH, 1978, DETAIL; PANNE VELVET; TRANSFER PRINT, COLOR XEROX; FULL PIECE 90 BY 50 INCHES.

WOMEN'S WEAR, 1988, DETAIL; HAND-MADE PAPER, COLOR COPY, PATCH-WORK; FULL PIECE 50 BY 20 INCHES.

BOARDWALK II, 1990; RICE PAPER LAMINATED ON GOURD; PHOTOCOPY, HEAT TRANSFER; SIZE.

G L E N
K A U F M A N

Pattern and image on and into the fabric surface have been a part of my life as an artist and educator for many years. These two aspects have been intertwined in mutually stimulating ways to the benefit of both. My work in surface design has relied primarily on photographic processes to transfer images to the fabric surface, bringing to the work something of the "real" world with the intent of transformation. In instances of printing the pattern or image, it lays on the fabric. When I use shibori techniques, the dye penetrates through the fabric. In each case a "design" that hovers near the surface is created. The processes employed, and their unique results, are an integral aspect of each work.

My early involvement in the 1950s, with what was later coined surface design, was with screen printing on paper and repeat design on fabric. Although the emphasis in my graduate study was on weaving, I was also intrigued with the possibilities of printed design with pigments on the fabric surface. Later I had the opportunity to study in Copenhagen, Denmark, where I was first introduced to the exciting prospect of printing dye into the fabric surface. This technology, which allowed intensity of color with softness of hand, was common in the art schools of Europe as well as in the textile industry.

While I was head of textiles at Cranbrook Academy of Art, I met Meda Parker Johnston, a student in the Design Department with a burning

GLOVE FALLING FROM SEVENTH HEAVEN, 1984; SILK, WOOL, NATURAL DYES; SHIBORI; 13-3/4 BY 10-3/4 INCHES.

desire to explore the potentials of dye and fabric. I welcomed her into the textile studio and we soon embarked on a collaboration that resulted in our co-authorship of *Design on Fabrics*. Although we worked on a variety of processes of dyeing and printing for the book, my studio work at the time focused on woven and non-woven structures.

Subsequently I moved to the University of Georgia in Athens where I established a program in weaving and surface design, continuing my own work in structure using manmade materials to create a variety of garment-inspired forms. It is there I began work on the glove as object and symbol, continuing that focus for over ten years. The final phase, completed in 1984 in Japan, was a series of representations of gloves executed in stitch resist shibori. Gloves became spacecraft, juxtaposed with celestial bodies in an indigo night sky or floating among Jacquard-patterned clouds.

BUILDING THE GREAT WALL WAS ONLY A PARTIAL SOLUTION TO THE FREQUENT RAIDS AND PILLAGING OF CHINESE CITIES BY CENTRAL ASIATIC NOMADS. BEGINNING WITH THE SHANG ERA, 1766-1122 B.C., EMPERORS BEGAN SENDING VAST QUANTITIES OF FOOD, GOLD, AND ESPECIALLY SILKS AS GIFTS TO KEEP THE PEACE.

Since the early 1980s, I have spent a part of each year working in a succession of studios in Japan. I have executed work that has employed photographic images, in gold or silver leaf, of landscapes, traditional and contemporary architecture from Japan, America, and Korea that float behind grids on silk panels. These images are glimpses of my world as seen through the view finder, a window, or a lattice. My visual world is perceived through this grid, isolating an image or series of images. I want the grid to create an illusion of space, with the viewer, the grid, and the essential image each occupying sequential planes in a visual construct.

The works since the mid-eighties are intended to be a synthesis of Asia and America in both an aesthetic and a technical sense. The challenge I have taken on is how to document place, how to record and preserve a visual world in flux that has had an impact on me, how to retell my encounters and travels in America and Asia. I have chosen the screen printed image, precious metal leaf, and silk fabric as the means and media to express my inner vision of the outer world. They represent a technology of the West and materials of the East, and thus enhance the theme of synthesis in my work.

In the fabric surface lives the experience.

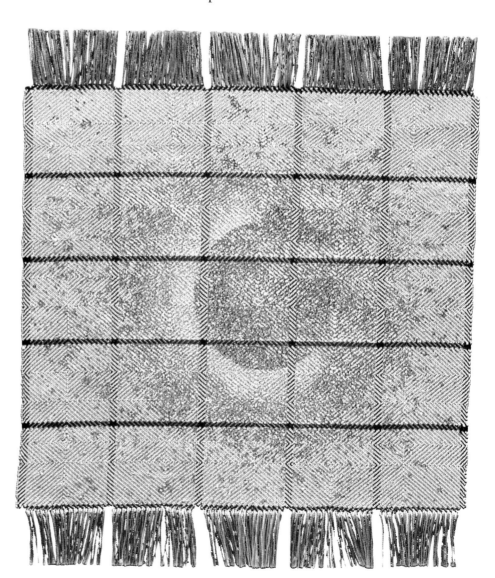

GALAXY HERCULES, 1985; SILK, SILVER LEAF; TWILL WEAVE, SCREEN PRINT, EMBROIDERY; 7-3/4 BY 6-3/4 INCHES. PHOTO: T. HATAKEYAMA.

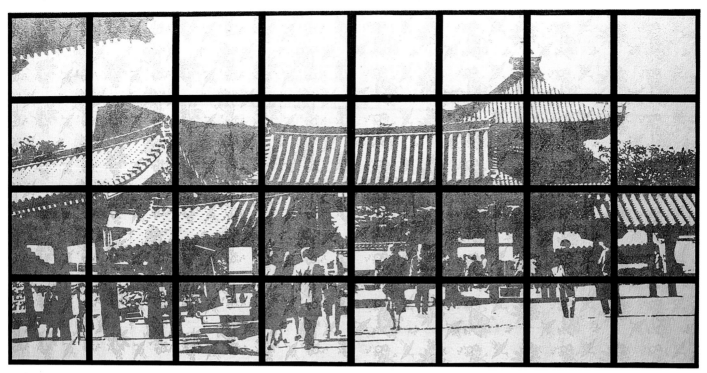

TOFUKUJI, 1990; SILK DAMASK, SILVER LEAF; SCREEN PRINT; 24 BY 48 INCHES. PHOTO: A. KOIKE.

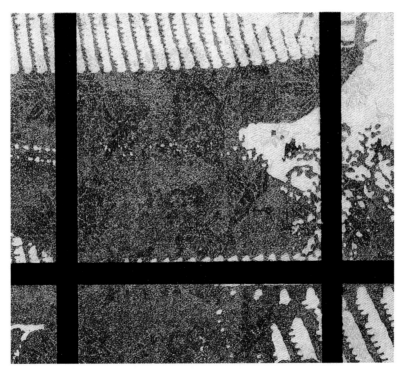

TOFUKUJI, DETAIL.

SPACE WINDOWS/INSADONG, 1991; SILK DAMASK, SILVER LEAF; SCREEN PRINT; EACH PANEL 24 BY 24 INCHES. PHOTO: T. KANASAKI.

PULGUK-SA, KYONG-KU, 1990; SILK
DAMASK, SILVER LEAF; SCREEN PRINT;
48 BY 24 INCHES. PHOTO: A. KOIKE.

YOSHIKAWA, NOTO, 1990; SILK DAMASK, SILVER LEAF; SCREEN PRINT; 48 BY 24 INCHES. PHOTO: A. KOIKE.

AMERICAN TOTEMS, 1987; SILK, SILVER LEAF; JACQUARD WEAVE, SCREEN PRINT; EACH PANEL 71 BY 28 INCHES. PHOTO: T. HATAKEYAMA.

VICTORIA
RIVERS

If I were a bowerbird from Australia, then I could say that I came by my love of shining things genetically. Since I am not, I will blame this attraction on my Taunte, my father's great-aunt.

She was a vibrant, adventuresome woman who struck out on her own, going from Louisville, Kentucky to New York City to become a hat designer in the early 1900s. When she was in her seventies and I was four, she would let me create deliberate runs and holes in her stockings while she wore them. While my mother and she sipped on a surreptitious bit of Mogen David wine she kept tucked away in her dresser drawer, I would color under my fingernails, like all proper Louisville ladies did then, with her white pencil and rearrange the lavender-white hair she saved in her hair receiver. But best of all, Taunte had saved "things" for me from her hat making days: three-foot-long pheasant feathers, clusters of bird of paradise feathers, sequins and rhinestones, bits of curly Persian lamb fur, a real Spanish mantilla and such.

My parents recognized that I was "creative," but my handiwork was not always appreciated. One day after a Brownie Scout meeting, I decided to spiff up a beige wool carpet at home—painting watercolor designs and splatters all over the rug. I just could not understand my parents' lack of enthusiasm for this obvious improvement, but maybe I should have recalled the time I cut squares out of the drapes with my first pair of scissors.

SELF PORTRAIT, FANTASY I, 1978-79; VELVETEEN, DYE; 35 BY 39 INCHES.
PHOTO COURTESY THE ARTIST.

When it was time for university, my fondest fantasy was to become an entomologist, to crawl around in the Amazon forest looking for exotic beetles. But my parents insisted that I study art. My undergraduate work focused on printmaking, specifically screen printing, and in graduate school I became interested in textile printing and dyeing. I approached screen printing on cloth much like I had printing on paper, only I made one-of-a-kind images instead of multiples. The early works were not in repeat, and I treated them like paintings that I worked back into with quilting, padding, ribbon, metallic ribbon applique, and streaks and splashes of sewn-on glass beads.

After I finished school in Kentucky, I taught studio arts for six years at a community college in Tennessee. During the summers I would work intensively making large, overlapping, padded shapes with screen printed, hand painted, airbrushed, and beaded imagery. Basically, my creative process consisted of lying in bed at night, trying to sleep, but seeing images in my head instead. Often, I would get up late at night to sketch out what I "saw." I would develop those rough sketches, using notes I had written in the margins to help me remember what I imagined.

IN PERSIA AROUND 2000 B.C., SMALL METAL PLAQUES OF GOLD, SILVER, OR BRONZE, RANGING FROM A QUARTER OF AN INCH TO FOUR INCHES IN DIAMETER, WERE SEWN ONTO CLOTH IN REGULAR PATTERNS.

PENLAND, 1990; CLOTH, DYES, JEWELS,
GLITTER, IRIDESCENT AND FLUORESCENT
PIGMENTS; 72 BY 28 INCHES. PHOTO:
JAMES WOODSON.

At this time I was reading a lot of metaphysical literature and writings
by Carl Jung. I felt that my imagery was a gift from the collective
unconscious, and this was the underlying theme of works from this period.
Those sketches would serve as a guide in executing the printed piece,
since white cotton velveteen is like white paper, and fiber reactive dyes are
transparent like watercolor. I was displeased with how flat the dye could
look, so I started scratching back into wet dye to rough up the velveteen's
nap and to unevenly distribute the color. When the dyed imagery was
complete, I would heat set the dyes with an iron and wash the piece.
After the extra dye was removed and the fabric returned to a soft hand,
I sewed into it with glass beads and appliqued satin ribbons or three-
dimensional dyed cloth. I wanted to enrich and enliven the fabric by
altering how light would play on its surface. At the time I was barely
conscious of my motivations, but I now see that these various steps led
to using painted neon light with the cloth.

My work has changed dramatically since moving to Sacramento in 1980,
and I welcome these changes, traumatic as they sometimes have been.
A creative person must constantly grow; I have little respect for artists who
find a comfortable niche and stay in it because they are known for "their
thing." In the mid-1980s, I stopped working with fabric. I began to draw
again, to work with sheet lead, found objects, black light, and was making
constructed pieces. From that hiatus, I was able to start with a fresh perspective and decide what I wanted to toss out and what I wanted to keep. I got
the idea to use neon light and from there developed a way of painting on it
to integrate it with the cloth's imagery. I spent a number of years learning to
control the light and to deal with technical aspects of mounting the trans-
formers and wiring, and developing lighter weight fiber glass structures.

New images came about from a fertile trip to Asia, where things I saw and
experienced helped me get some perspective on surface and light. The body

of work after that trip consists of large pieces with intensively worked beaded, jewelled, and appliqued surfaces, with sometimes up to three hundred hours of hand sewing. I received a lot of help from student assistants on the sewing; otherwise, I could never have completed as many pieces as I did.

Much of my work deals with self-remembering—that is, of recalling that we are united with all living things. Through exaggerated scenarios from nature, I attempt to play on concepts of the sublime to evoke feelings of being and belonging in the universe. I use images that are within a familiar context to allow the viewer to find her or his own spiritual validation.

The textile work of indigenous peoples, from Asia especially, continues to inspire me. The inherent language in the material culture of textiles and the ways that textiles and costumes are integrated into the social and ritual lives of their makers are of great importance. In 1992 I was in India studying textiles that use light-reflective materials, including those using iridescent beetle wings. Now I am on a path researching metallic and iridescent beetles and how these have been used in personal adornment around the world. I plan to integrate them into my textile work as well.

Even though I'm not crawling around the jungle looking for bugs, I do see that a small part of my life's dream has come full circle—integrating the study of beetles with what I love now. I haven't wanted to cut up any curtains yet, but who knows? I just got a new pair of scissors.

BLUE HOLE, 1990; CLOTH, JEWELS, DYES, FLUORESCENT AND IRIDESCENT PIGMENTS; 72 BY 33 INCHES. PHOTO: ROBERT DI FRANCO.

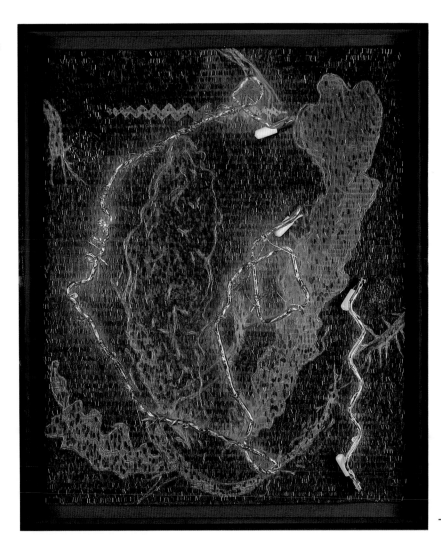

BLOODLINES, 1989; CLOTH, DYES, BEADS, OIL PIGMENTS, NEON; PAINTED; 46 BY 39 INCHES. PHOTO: JAMES WOODSON.

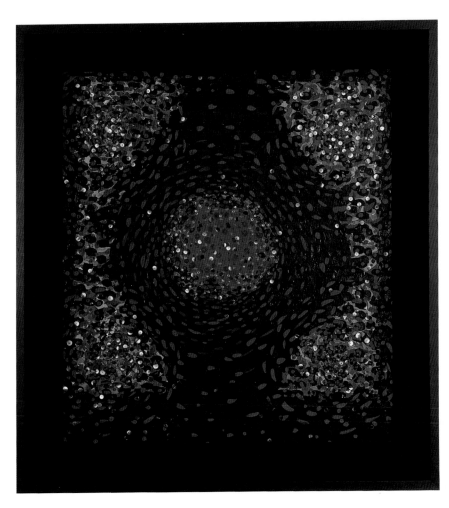

MAGNETISM, 1992; CLOTH, SEQUINS, BEETLE WING PIECES, INTERFERENCE PLASTIC; SCREEN PRINTED, PAINTED. PHOTO: ROBERT DI FRANCO.

NIGHT GARDEN, 1989; CLOTH, DYES, GLITTER AND IRIDESCENT PIGMENTS, BEADS; 96 BY 30 INCHES. PHOTO: JAMES WOODSON.

NIGHT GARDEN, DETAIL.

GILI TRAWANGAN, 1988; SUEDE, DYES, IRIDESCENT AND GLITTER PIGMENTS, IRIDESCENT SNAKESKIN; APPLIQUE; 48 BY 33 INCHES. PHOTO: JAMES WOODSON.

AMRITSAR, 1989; RADIANCE FABRIC, JEWELS, BEADS, DYES, PIGMENTS, IRIDESCENT SNAKESKIN; APPLIQUE; 48 BY 32 INCHES. PHOTO: JAMES WOODSON.

JUNCO SATO
POLLACK

What motivates me to create is a moment of sublime experience of finding beauty in life. Finding a seashell on a beach and discovering the fragile yet powerful beauty of seashells freshly washed up on the beach motivated me to produce the "Sea Creatures" and "Bivalves" series. Studying a group of treasured tea bowls and being deeply struck by the congealed beauty of the forms and surfaces prompted me to carry my creation into the "Vessel" series.

Discovering beauty in certain things comes from everyday activities, too. Living in a house covered with ivy vines, I observed daily the leaves framing the window and how light filtered through them. This experience gave me an opportunity to develop a series of warp print and silkscreened fabrics combined with patterning by multi-harness weaving, shibori, and silver leaf.

Ideas for creation come from intellectual research on cultural matters as well. Sometimes I find myself making connections between separate things that interest me as topics of research, and all of a sudden things start to unravel and interconnect. Through my research on zen painting, calligraphy, Eastern and Western architecture, gardens, and cultures in general, I discovered that connections can be made between the forms and styles of calligraphy and manners of abstraction in drawing, and in Eastern and Western landscape painting.

GRAPE IVY SCROLL, 1989; SILK, SILVER, SILVER LEAF; WOVEN, WARP PRINT, SATIN DAMASK; 27 BY 70 INCHES. SCROLL SERIES.

9 1

THE EARLIEST
FIND OF
METALLIC
EMBROIDERY
WAS MADE
UNDER LAYERS
OF ICE IN A
FIFTH-CENTURY
B.C. TOMB.
THE SITE OF
PAZYRYK, NORTH
OF WHERE
MONGOLIA,
CHINA, AND THE
FORMER USSR
MEET, YIELDED
GOLD-COVERED
WOODEN
BUTTONS AND
BELTS TRIMMED
WITH ROWS OF
STITCHES DONE
IN SINEW THREAD
WRAPPED WITH
FINE STRIPS
OF TINFOIL.

These studies led to the "Scroll" and "Screen" series. When the subject is large and broad, I need to simplify, to work out each point in a very logically progressive manner as if I were producing a thesis. I methodically lay out and develop my "discussion," progressing to the point I want to make. The way I work is time consuming, but like anything in life, good things don't come easily. Skills take time to ferment and mature. There are things that simply cannot be produced in large numbers.

My vocabulary of expression involves the entire textile medium and techniques available. I work from obtaining the right material to produce fabric (including growing silk worms and reeling out filaments) with which I embellish and create textural surfaces. The materials I favor are silk and polyester for their fineness, luster, and thermoplastic nature, and silver and gold for the light-reflecting richness they create. The metal is finely drawn and flattened, or flattened and finely slit to be made into a yarn by twisting around the silk filament core, and then it is colored and woven into gossamer fabric.

While I weave with silk and metal threads, images are either painted or printed on the warp, so that the layering of patterning is integrated on the surface. After the fabric is woven, then metal leaf, painting, shibori, or machine embroidery is utilized on the surface. Layering images in this way, I can take a painterly approach and combine a variety of subtle textures on the fabric. To form a sculpture, stitch-binding threads are integrated as I weave the fabric. Then I gather up or bind the fabric after it is woven. The wrinkles from gathering or binding give the fabric an elasticity that enables it to be formed into sculpture. While I find both approaches (painterly and sculptural) are essential to my work, it is important to separate issues so that I maintain clarity in my focus.

KANZAN-COLD MOUNTAIN, 1992; SILK, ACRYLIC PAINT, SILVER; HEAT PRESS, AIRBRUSH, MACHINE STITCHING; 85 BY 110 INCHES. SCROLL SERIES.

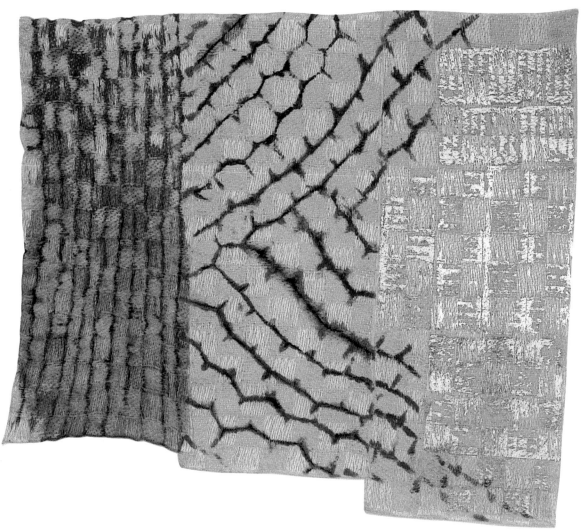

TRIPTYCH: WINTER, 1991; RAYON, COTTON, GOLD LEAF; SATIN DAMASK, SHIBORI; 29 BY 33 INCHES. SCREEN SERIES.

My recent work involves my interpretation of aesthetics. By embracing rather than rejecting the styles and skills of the past, I am interpreting the aesthetic ideals of Japanese culture that I grew up with and studied, such as noh theater, tea ceremony, calligraphy, poetry, gardens, et cetera. I am studying the aesthetic of Japanese picture scrolls and screen paintings and reinterpreting it in the "Screen" and "Scroll" series. Metallic light reflective surface also plays a large part in these works.

Grape Ivy Scroll is warp-printed and woven in satin damask patterning. The imagery is repeated in silver leaf, *surihaku,* applied on the fabric. **Frost Venus I**, **II**, and **III** and **KANZAN** represent a level of abstraction toward the rounded cursive, *gyosho* style of expression, taking nature, landscape, or figures as subject matter. Here, the relationship of drawing and calligraphy begins a visual interplay with fabric. The drawing is done in fabric by making creases or folds and heat setting them permanently, then airbrushing to set off the layered images against transparent fabric ground. The shadows of the pieces on the wall create reverse images, adding to the sculptural nature of the work. Metallic stitches run in grids, keeping the folds in place against the weight of fabric as well as providing graphic structure.

ANGEL WINGS, 1984; SILK; WOVEN, SHIBORI; 12 INCHES EACH. BIVALVE SERIES.

Sometimes I work solidly on one series, but most of the time I work on various series simultaneously, as each feeds ideas to the other. I enjoy making objects, but I am also interested in developing ideas and in the challenge of problem solving each idea brings. If the first piece does not completely say what I am trying to say, another one is developed as a criticism to it, with the result being that a series develops.

Weaving restricted me physically—having to stay in my studio—and it was time consuming. Shibori is portable and I carry it with me on my trips. Voluminous amounts of fabric can be packed into a small case. The time it took to manufacture fabric limited my ability to produce, but I have found a factory in Lyon, France that can produce gossamer fabric for me in silver and silk. This is changing the scale and the way I work.

DANCER #2, 1992; SILVER, SILK; WOVEN, SHIBORI, CONSTRUCTED; 15 BY 15 BY 15 INCHES. VESSEL SERIES.

FROST VENUS II, 1992; SILK, ACRYLIC PAINT, SILVER; HEAT PRESS, AIRBRUSH, MACHINE STITCHING; 24 BY 15 BY 15 INCHES. SCROLL SERIES.

J A C Q U E L I N E
T R E L O A R

In 1969 I left art college in London, England and went to live twelve years in northern Italy where I designed for textile printers and stylists. I was fortunate to work with people responsible for producing some of the most fabulous textiles in the modern world. Their understanding of a fabric's qualities and possibilities, plus an absolute mandate for excellence, is a debt I acknowledge by creating my pieces.

By the mid-1980s I was living in Toronto, drawing and painting silk scarves. My first non-wearables were a result of an instinctive desire to further explore the medium. This is generally how my work progresses— from instinct and emotion. I attach to an idea or an image and, according to how it affects me, it is transformed by the medium. The pieces are usually complex, both physically and narratively. They require sustained interest and commitment.

I am fascinated by ritual and pageantry, particularly when I encounter the stories of people who have crossed oceans and continents, leaving behind material possessions and family, yet bringing with them their legends and their history. Their stories often translate into elaborate structures with curious songs and dances, the origins of which are as old as the lands from where they came. The power of these stories enacted is almost physical for me and I seek to recreate them as best I can.

DAPHNE AND APOLLO, 1988, DETAIL; DUPPIONI SILK, FABRIC PAINT, BEADS; PAINTING, EMBELLISHMENT; FULL PIECE 36 BY 48 INCHES.

Performance has been an important contemporary resource for me. I regularly photograph dance, theater, circuses, and all sorts of puppet and marionette shows. These highly evocative events regularly merge together with my passion for the statuary and architecture of the Italian baroque period. Within this area are references to the garden, the grotto, the palace, the church, and the sculpture fresco and stucco work which was such an integral part of these structures. The research for the pieces is a time consuming yet fascinating aspect of the work. Also, I end up with an extensive amount of knowledge on the most disparate subject matter. Commissions have resulted in research on the Lippizaner stallions, the origins of the Trevi fountain, the early Venetian Republic, and the history of terrestrial and astrological maps.

A FINE FRESCO SHOWING TWO WOMEN AND A MAN, ALL CLAD IN BRIEF LOINCLOTHS, AND DOING ACROBATICS ACROSS THE BACK OF A CHARGING BULL, WAS UNEARTHED FROM A SITE ON CRETE DATED AT 1400-1200 B.C.

Currently, I am working on a project which has as part of its basis the 18th-century Italian presepio, or Christmas crib. Important examples are housed in the Abbey of San Martino in Naples. Artisans of all categories were employed to create room-sized miniature villages and scenes portraying their colorful city, from ruins to shop fronts, from foreign potentates to local urchins. The pieces number in the hundreds. A typical figurine would be no more than ten inches high, with moulded and polychromed features and limbs. The garments are perfectly made and embellished according to the status of the bearer. The perfection of these figures is such that they have served as a vital source of information regarding the dress and popular costume of the period. My friends were invited to a "presepio party," with notes and instructions as to how to transform themselves into shepherds, magicians, acrobats, and figures of the court and church. I awaited them with my camera.

My studio table is piled with those photos and an assortment of metallic tassels and braids. To one side is a heap of metal findings and strange, small castings of moveable clowns and bits of wings and cupids. A collection of woven baskets holds feathers, artificial flowers, and an assortment of colored pens and pencils. On the far wall to my left is an eight-by-eight-foot plywood board on which I do most of my large pieces. It holds a drape of nylon which is painted with the beginning forms of two colorful, almost abstract dancers.

It is an enormous privilege to continue to create. It is frequently challenging, at times almost crushingly so, but it permits me growth and others, I hope, joy.

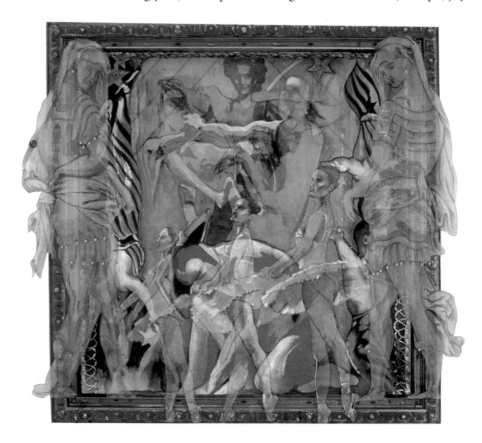

PERFORMANCE SUMMER, 1989; DUPPIONI AND ORGANZA SILKS, NYLON, FABRIC PAINT, POLYESTER FILM, BEADS; PAINTING, EMBELLISHMENT; 48 BY 48 INCHES. PHOTO: ALLISON OULLETTE.

THE RETURN OF ULYSSES, 1989; DUPPIONI AND ORGANZA SILKS, CANVAS, BEADS, RIBBONS, FABRIC PAINT; HEAT TRANSFER, PAINTING, EMBELLISHMENT; 66 BY 78 INCHES. PHOTO: ALLISON OULLETTE.

THE PROCESSION, 1990; NYLON, ACRYLIC AND FABRIC PAINT, BEADS; APPLIQUE, PAINTING, HEAT TRANSFER; 144 BY 84 INCHES. PHOTO: KEN HERDY.

L E N O R E
D A V I S

My mother gave me and my sister the family tradition of enjoying working with fabric in an environment where mistakes were greeted warmly and process was as significant as product. I want to thank her.

We spent long hours sewing, ended up with products and by-products, and started on more, anticipating pleasure. Another childhood passion shared with my family was for musicals. My sister and I produced vaudeville-like shows and organized circuses with the neighbors. We used all household resources and wildly enjoyed the preparation and the performances. Drawing and painting became an essential escape as important as sewing and working with fabric. I remember the first time I was called out of class in grade school to paint trees in the hallway, and how I loved it.

The feeling of getting out of "class" to paint still returns to me now, as a studio artist. My studio is in a commercial building within easy walking distance of my home. I share it with another fabric artist who, like myself, struggles in the grown-up world of making a living with craft and bearing responsibilities of the full scenario of process.

The making of two-dimensional fabric pieces is the "painting" part of my life; a combination of cloth, needlework, printmaking, and painting, in a format that can hold complex ideas. Often I do not have time to plan my two-dimensional works in detail. I start somewhere in the middle, a theme

develops, and resolution is reached. This is a risk worth taking. It appeals to my spontaneity and fond reliance on familiar tools to make beautiful marks. Earlier, as a ceramicist, the marks of the brush on the round surfaces were a constant fascination. They were done once and retouched. Brushing dye or paint on fabric is related, but the addition of printmaking techniques expands my repertoire.

An interest in human gesture and motion keeps me returning to making fabric figures. They are both sculpture and dolls; they are beings in my imagination, or wishes. Perhaps I was a dancer or acrobat in a previous life. Now as a closet performer lusting for center stage, it is my figures that perform, love the spotlight, and capture the hearts of the viewers.

Teaching workshops has long been a favorite part of my business. I meet people from many regions, share what is personally a pleasure, and get a

IN THE OLD PALACE SITE ON CRETE, CA. 1800-1600 B.C., A SWORD WITH AN ACROBAT ENGRAVED ON ITS HILT WAS DISCOVERED. THE ACROBAT IS DEPICTED WEARING A SHORT, PATTERNED SKIRT.

sense of the universal needs and abilities of women. There is power expressed in these classes, a sense of personal independence, and the participants revel in the environment of intense work.

My penchant for options and special projects gives me the variety I need in my life. Sometimes it gets out of hand and I am overwhelmed as several projects collide, and I spin around seeking a focal point. I have called for help more than once—to my husband, also an artist, and to people in the fiber community. They all have my thanks for getting me through the bad times.

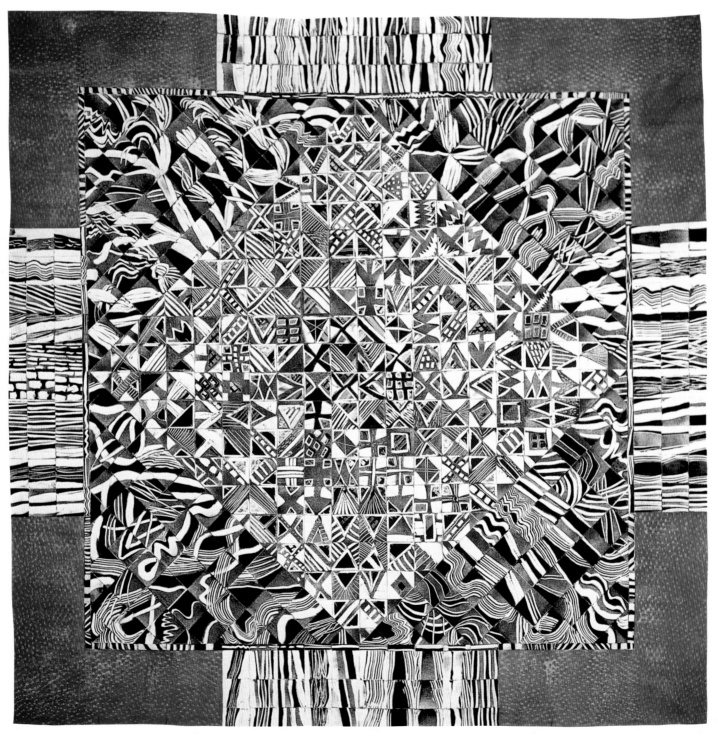

DIAMOND CONSTELLATION, 1992; COTTON, TEXTILE PAINT; MONOTYPE, REVERSE APPLIQUE, MACHINE STITCHING; 58 BY 58 INCHES.

103

ESCAPE OVER WORK MOUNTAINS, 1987; COTTON,
TEXTILE PAINT; 60 BY 60 INCHES.

DIAMOND AND CROSS AND DETAIL, 1992; COTTON VELVETEEN, TEXTILE PAINT, DYE, METALLIC THREAD; MONOTYPE, PAINTING, QUILTING; 56 BY 56 INCHES.

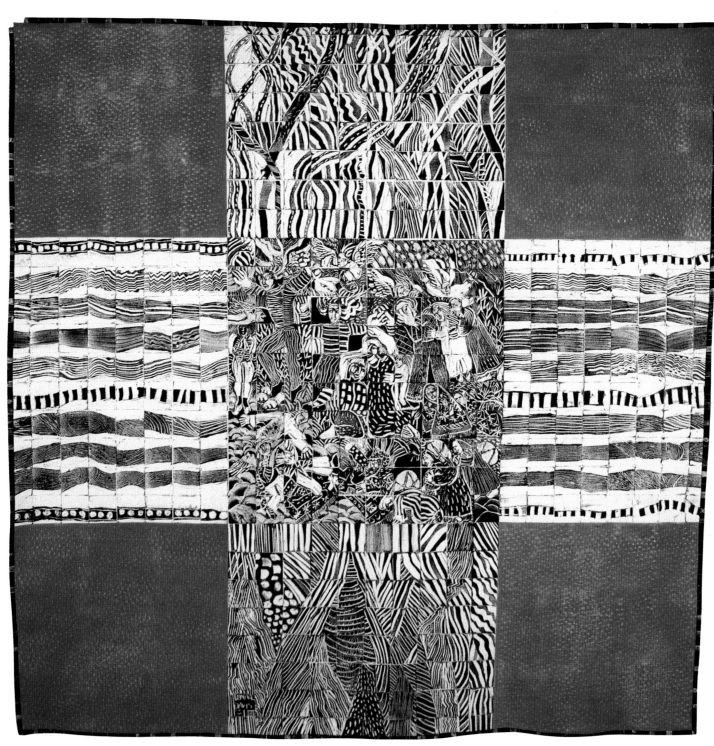

NOT ENOUGH GUARDIAN ANGELS, 1991; COTTON, TEXTILE PAINT; MONOTYPE; 58 BY 58 INCHES.

NICK
CAVE

The artist's duty is to alleviate any misconceptions his audience might harbor toward his art and to guide them on an exploration of the work. My connection to the world is through my art, where I attempt to open the viewers/participants to their inner selves so they can see and relate to the world with a broader clarity and vision.

Pattern on fabric means more to me than design. The flat, single-plane surface can also be draped in an interior space, on a human figure, or cut up and reassembled in a variety of ways. The traditionally two-dimensional feature of surface design is capable of producing excitement, tension, and agitation as it is made an element of theater. My personal intrigue is to remove materials from their familiar roles and parade them into a new condition.

My performance is not mere demonstration. Rather, it is about the possibilities of transformation in an individual and a healthy exploration of what an individual consists of. Transformation is a quasi-religious idea, suggesting transfiguration and transubstantiation, involving belief and disbelief. It is also a concept of science fiction, which employs invented materials, objects, and creatures and the fantasy transformations of the human body into other, altered states.

I believe that the familiar must move toward the fantastic. Allowing the artist to lavish attention on an object can be a way of giving life to inner

UNTITLED DRAWING, 1989-90; PURE PIGMENTS, MIXED MEDIA; 48 BY 60 INCHES.

107

experiences and emotions. I want to evoke feelings that are unnamed, that are not realized except in dreams.

With a background in African and modern dance, I've been able to experience expression, spiritual encounter, and emotions by moving through space. Both positive and negative space play equal roles in setting up emotion and activity between the figure and space. A similar contemplation occurs between two individuals and their surroundings. My work arbitrates contemporary social, political, and personal issues. I investigate primal states deeply ingrained, yet distilled through a cultural haze into emotions. I seek out the tensions and contradictions between intense reality and interpreted reality. My objective is to plunge resolutely and deeply into my subconscious, to lift my feelings and motivations, and, in the process, transform them in an intuitive manner.

A FRESCO OF A FIGURE DANCING IN A GARDEN WAS FOUND IN THE HAGIA TRIADA [1400-1200 B.C.] DIG ON CRETE. THE COSTUME HAS A FLOUNCED, DIVIDED SKIRT MADE OF TWIN LAYERS OF COLORED RECTANGLES, ALTERNATING WITH WIDE LAYERS OF FIGURED MATERIAL.

Materials give form to inward experiences and help me find and define my coexistence with, and relationship to, the world. I want to present a new view in which performance, dance, light, sound, and costume become a viable art form.

Any account I present about me or my work would be incomplete without referring to my mother, Sharron Kelly. She nourished me with a vision that is peripheral and a soul that is becoming gold. Thank you, mother.

UNTITLED, DETAIL.

UNTITLED, 1989-90; COTTON, PLASTIC, WOOD; FIBER REACTIVE DYE, PAINT, APPLIQUE; 60 BY 108 INCHES.

SOUND SUIT SERIES, 1992; PERFORMANCE COSTUMES. PHOTOS: JORGE GARCIA.

YARDAGE, 1991; SILK; DIRECT PAINTING.

YARDAGE, 1991, DETAIL; SILK; DIRECT PAINTING.

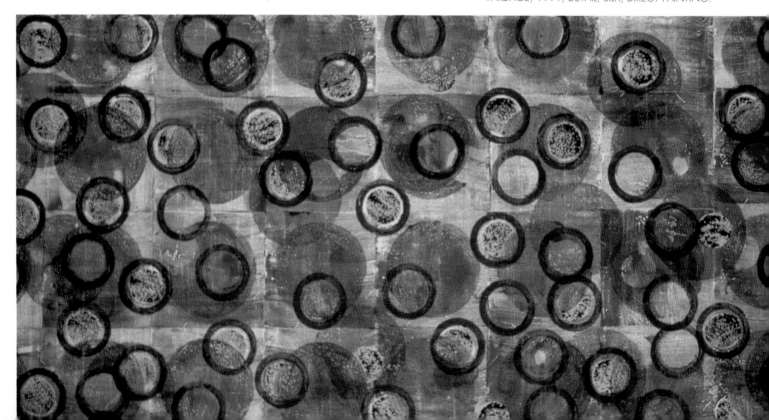

UNTITLED DRAWING, 1989-90; PURE PIGMENTS; MIXED MEDIA; 60 BY 72 INCHES.

D O R O T H Y
C A L D W E L L

I think that I've always been attracted to textiles. I grew up watching my mother dye wool for the rugs that she made, and enjoying the patterned squares of my great grandmother's pieced quilt that was on my bed. These kinds of things did not exist in the art school where I studied painting and sculpture.

It has been a slow journey back to retrieve and acknowledge those important early experiences with cloth. An object that helped in rediscovering my affinity to fabric was a small hand painted pillow by Lenore Davis, shown at the 1974 World Crafts Council exhibition in Toronto. The piece was called **Garden of Eden** and was a spoof on those black velvet tourist paintings. It was soft and humorous and so different from the hard edged work I'd been exposed to up until then. This piece formed a bridge for me between painting and textiles.

Because I had no technical training in textiles, I came in through the back door. Initially my dyes washed out and the wax didn't hold up. This led to working with basic materials that did not require much technical expertise. Wax resist and discharged cotton are not precious materials, and using them gives me the freedom to experiment. I often begin by covering the cloth with a patterned or textured surface. This gives me a ground to work on, and the process helps remove the creative blocks I sometimes experience about getting started. Repeating a shape or motion is a gentle way to move into a piece, and doing something with my hands frees up my ideas in a way

TOWER, 1984; DISCHARGED COTTON, INDIGO; BLOCK PRINTED WAX RESIST, PAINTED, STITCHED, DYED; 36 BY 120 INCHES. PHOTO: DAVID SALTMARCHE.

that planning and thinking do not. I enjoy this building process that seems to collect and evoke time. Marks made through repetition, like the curve scored in the floor where the door was swept back and forth for years, intrigue me. I also enjoy the physical movement of printing and stamping and how it seems like a record of human rhythms and variations.

Traditional textiles give me a lot of pleasure and I can't resist buying and collecting them. For many years, I have felt a strong connection to African textiles. I appreciate the cloth's boldness and the way the artisans incorporate the new influences, imagery, and materials that come their way. Spots, blobs, and irregularities, rather than being considered mistakes, are integrated into the design, adding an element of surprise to the surface. I've adopted this approach to my own work.

WHEREVER WE CATCH A GLIMPSE OF CENTRAL EUROPEAN CLOTHS, THEY ARE FANCY. THE NEOLITHIC AGE CLOTHS FROM SWITZERLAND AND GERMANY HAVE STRIPES, TRIANGLES, CHECKS AND ELABORATE BORDERS.

I have lived in rural Ontario since 1972. I enjoy the seclusion and connections to the landscape: the dark and light patterns of the first snow as it rests on the furrows of plowed fields; the spots of energy that reflect off the bland Ontario landscape; a patch of luminous green winter wheat; bright red dogwood along the edges of fields. My work is a reflection of my environment and the vehicle that connects me to all other aspects of my life.

DOGWOOD IN MARCH, 1988; DISCHARGED COTTON, GOLD LEAF; WAX RESIST, APPLIQUE, QUILTING; 20 BY 22 INCHES. PHOTO: DAN MYERS.

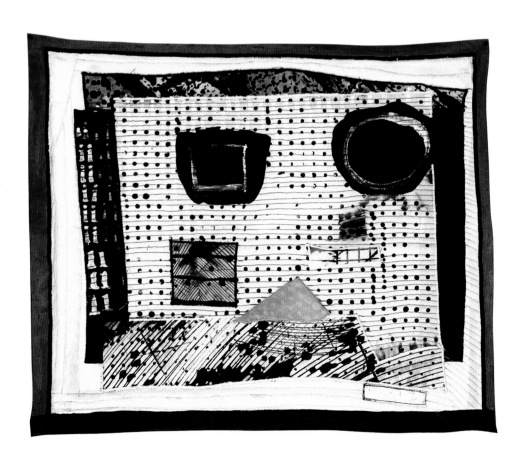

RING AROUND THE MOON, 1989; DISCHARGED COTTON, ACRYLICS; WAX RESIST, APPLIQUE, QUILTING; 18 BY 22 INCHES. PHOTO: DAN MYERS.

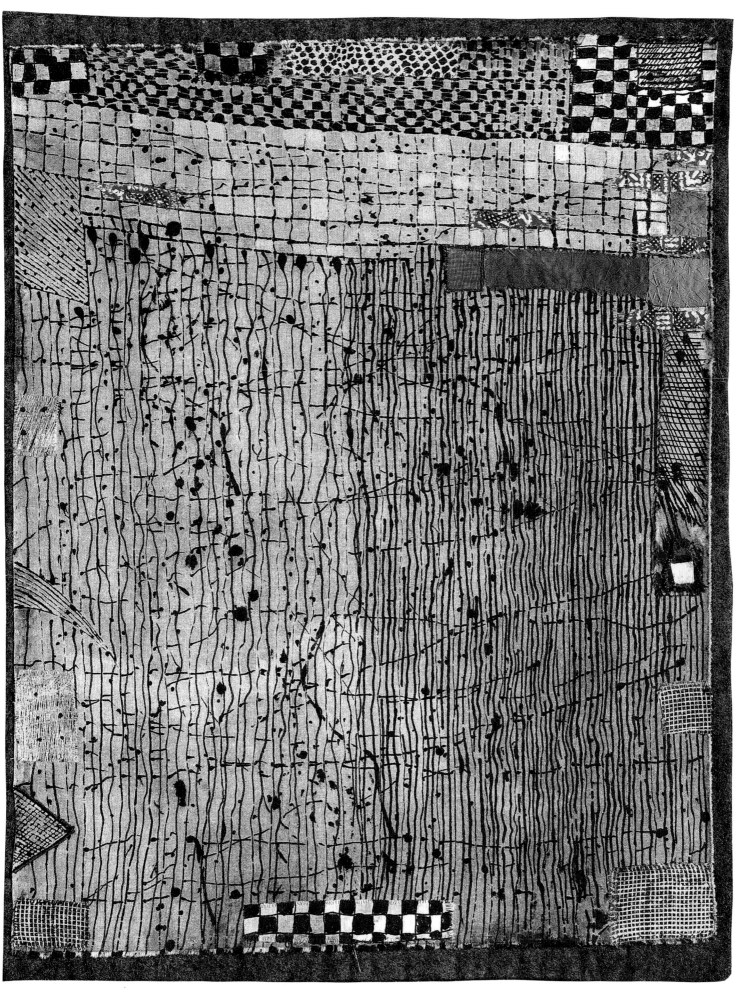

ALONE WITH THE TINKLING OF BELLS, 1991; DISCHARGED COTTON, GOLD LEAF; WAX RESIST, STITCHING, APPLIQUE; 18 BY 22 INCHES.
PHOTO: THOMAS MOORE.

WILL THE MOON ALWAYS BE THERE?, 1991; DISCHARGED COTTON, GOLD LEAF; WAX RESIST, APPLIQUE, STITCHING; 18 BY 22 INCHES.
PHOTO: JOHN DEAN.

BETWEEN TWO, 1991; DISCHARGED COTTON, GOLD LEAF; WAX RESIST, APPLIQUE, STITCHING; 18 BY 22 INCHES. PHOTO: THOMAS MOORE.

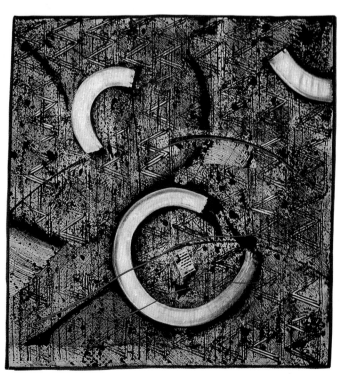

HOLE IN THE SKY, 1989; DISCHARGED COTTON, GOLD LEAF, STICKS; BATIK; 48 BY 48 INCHES. PHOTO: DAN MYERS.

S U S A N
W I L C H I N S

Textiles provide a breadth and flexibility of expression which make all other materials seem limited by comparison. They combine the texture and relief qualities of sculpture or pottery, the color range of paint, and the literal expressive potential of photography. There is little I cannot say effectively with a textile of some kind. Textiles also have a special personal resonance because they are tied to important early life and family experiences: hand-knitted clothing, embroidered linens, a tradition of quiltmaking among my female forebears, the feeling of cloth and thread in my hands. I find fabric work as natural as breathing and its expressions a "language" often more eloquent than English itself.

I began as a weaver. Weaving was magic. The cloth itself seemed to appear from nowhere, materializing before my eyes. My initial woven work was flat, clean, and geometric. Through experimentation with other woven structures, I began incorporating more relief and color. This led to a series of doubleweaves, with flaps protruding from the surface, enabling me to play with optical illusions.

Inspired by the works of Matisse, Klee, Vuillard, Klimt, and the Austrian painter Hundertwasser, I wanted to attain a sense of vitality in my work. Each of these artists' work expresses the differentiation—even the dissolution—of form through the juxtaposition of patterned objects and color. And each has a fluidity, a joy, I felt was missing in my work.

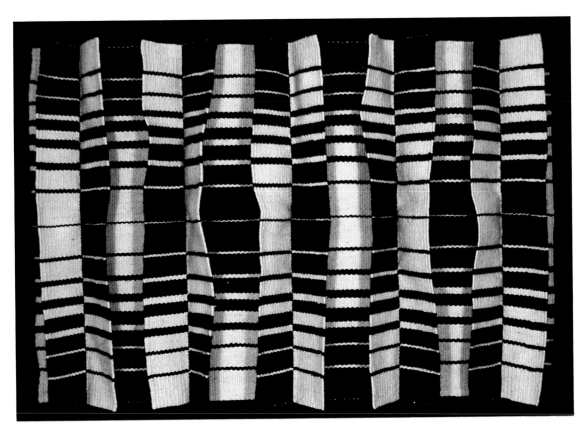

STUDY IN BLACK AND WHITE, 1978; WOOL WEFT, LINEN WARP; DOUBLEWEAVE; 36-3/4 BY 23-1/2 INCHES.

Frustrated by the limitations of the loom and its grid-like structure,
I began experimenting with dyed and pieced compositions, using flip-and-
sew piecing techniques. While I deliberately chose expressive instead of
realistic color, the pieces were still completely flat. I was working with
curved sections but still seeking to make a clean rectangular piece.
Sewing was often a nightmare.

I have always been fascinated with ambiguous imagery: the way in which
objects viewed from great distance or incredible closeness are rendered
abstract, and possibly unrecognizable. I studied satellite images, aerial
photography, maps, and microscopic sections of plant tissue. All of these
images ran together in my mind. In their beautiful abstraction they
seemed far more alike than different. I wanted to "do something" with
them in my work.

Trying to incorporate a feeling of texture, I began to work with collage.
I deliberately allowed dyes to bleed, tore exposed edges, exaggerated
colors, and incorporated a variety of stuffings, pleatings, and puckerings
in the assembly of the final piece.

After graduate school, I began experimenting intensively with screen printing. This led to screen printing over screen printing, stitching together

ELEVEN TINY
FAIENCE AND
GOLD BEADS AND
SOME REMNANTS
OF CLOTH WERE
FOUND IN A
TERRA-COTTA
BOX AT THE
TROY II, CA.
2500 B.C.,
DIG ON THE
AEGEAN SEA.

STREET LIGHTS, 1990; COTTON; SCREEN PRINTED, PIECED, APPLIQUED, STITCHED; 48 BY 72 INCHES.

layered strips or images from different printings, then placing more appliqued forms on top of these. This process combined the best aspects of everything I had tried before; it incorporated treasured historical techniques yet was entirely my own—something that constituted a "language" instead of just a "vocabulary." I was excited. The possibilities seemed endless.

In the warm, humid part of North Carolina where I live, the landscape was fragrant and thick with vining, trailing, flowering plants and trees. Working in my yard, I noticed soil texture, debris, all the little things that live, die, and fall around trees. I was also walking regularly in a local forest. When there, I always felt at peace. Forests are like cathedrals in their feeling of enclosed space and dappled light, of vibrant color but spiritual removal from worldly cares. I did a series of "forest floor" pieces, trying simultaneously to convey through vivid color my emotional response to the forest and to suggest with layered textures and composition the nature of the forest itself—its tactile quality and light, its synthesis of harmony and diversity, the exquisite details contained in its large spaces.

During this time I took note of other details. Every morning the wooden window shutters make patterns on my kitchen floor, shifting with the sun. I began to trace the patterns and elaborate on them, compiling a notebook of drawings: slats and rectangles, negative and positive space. I also collected photographs of surf, waves, shells. My recent work is a series of sea mantles based on experiences with the ocean, and a series of small pieces based on the window shutter light patterns. In the sea mantles, I try to emulate ocean colors and wave rhythms and, as in the forest pieces, to convey the intersection of tranquility with constant change. The window pieces are heavily beaded to suggest the dance and glitter of light reflections. Where stitching on my previous work was used almost solely for assembly of the work, the window pieces use machine and hand embroidery for mark making.

In a world where forests and oceans are despoiled by greed, where the sun itself becomes a source of sickness, I begin to feel like an archivist of disappearing things. We live, unfortunately, in a world where the simple attempt to celebrate nature's beauty is itself becoming a "statement."

INNER-SPACE ATLAS, PAGE 51, 1981; COTTON; DYED, PIECED, APPLIQUED, STITCHED; 55 BY 59-1/2 INCHES.

SEA MANTLE: COQUINA, 1992;
DYED, SCREEN PRINTED,
PIECED, APPLIQUED, STITCHED
FABRICS; 44 BY 53 INCHES.

SEA MANTLE: COQUINA, DETAIL.

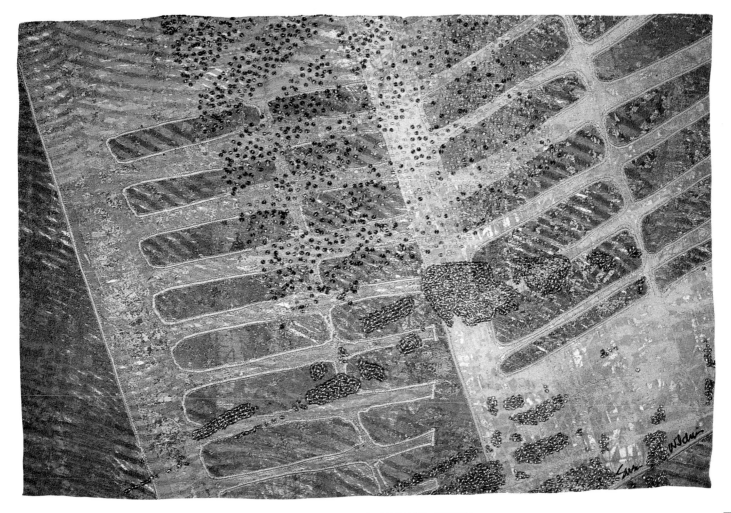

WINDOWS SERIES, #7, 1992; COTTON, BEADS; DYED, SCREEN PRINTED, APPLIQUED, REVERSE
APPLIQUED, MACHINE STITCHED, HAND EMBROIDERED; 11-1/4 BY 17 INCHES.

DEBORAH
FELIX

My first experience with surface design was in fifth grade while playing at a friend's house. It was around Easter and our resources were exhausted. We had ridden our minibikes until they were out of gas, and we then proceeded to pester her older brother until he banished us to the basement. In the basement, to our joy, we found Fred. Fred was a wonderful, docile white poodle that trusted us completely. Only after filling the sink with water, adding numerous drops of food coloring, and carefully reading the instructions on how to achieve the desired color did we find the solution to our boredom: a purple poodle.

When I was 14, my father was remarried, to an artist. I was thrown into a house with new sisters, a ceiling that was yellow, and a bathroom plastered with art prints. When you grow up in Buffalo, New York, you spend a lot of time indoors. I began to draw everything and anything in the house— chairs, plants, teapots, and my sisters. I still remember the expression on my stepmother's face when she discovered that I could draw. One afternoon she set up a still life in the kitchen with the intention of keeping six girls occupied. She set the timer for three minutes and told us to draw everything on the table. When the timer buzzed, I was officially a member of the family.

I went to college for art and came out with a degree in special education. My father's teaching side won out. In graduate school I discovered all the

HAWAIIAN DREAMS, 1983; DYED SILK, COTTON; BATIK, MACHINE APPLIQUE;
57 BY 82 INCHES.

bright, bold dyes that were available, and I began to make some
connection to those early kitchen drawings.

My life has gone through many changes—a marriage, a divorce, and
a remarriage—each event being chronicled by a new technique, new
materials, or a change in subject matter. There have been numerous
scenes, various haircuts, and telltale signs in my artwork that alluded to
where my life was or wasn't headed. Unfortunately, I'm not able to read
the message conveyed in each piece until long after it is completed.
I might have been able to save myself much personal strife.

Artmaking is embedded in my soul. I'm unable to do it as often as I like,
yet it is a motivating force. Recently I've gone back to teaching special
education. My father's side has won again. I've also learned that my
husband despises poodles; however, I'm working on convincing him that
we need a golden retriever. I hear they dye a wonderful shade of crimson.
All I need now is an accomplice.

RARE EXAMPLES
OF A SINGLE
PICTORIAL DESIGN
COVERING MOST
OF A TEXTILE,
FOUND IN AN
1800-1600 B.C.
SITE ON THE
ISLAND OF CRETE,
WERE INVENTIONS
OF THE PAINTERS,
AND WERE
INTENDED TO
IDENTIFY A DEITY
OR DIVINE
PRINCIPLE.

SAILOR'S DELIGHT, 1989; COMMERCIAL FABRIC, VINYL; PAINTING, REVERSE APPLIQUE; 91 BY 91 INCHES. PHOTO: ALAN WATSON.

DESERTED TROPICS, 1989; COMMERCIAL FABRIC, PASTELS, VINYL; PAINTING, REVERSE APPLIQUE; 120 BY 87 INCHES. PHOTO: ALAN WATSON.

OBJECTS OF LOVE, 1990; COMMERCIAL FABRIC, VINYL, PASTELS; PAINTING; 19 BY 6 FEET.

FLIGHT OF HAMMER AND BRUSH, 1992; COMMERCIAL FABRIC, VINYL, PASTELS; PAINTING;
8 BY 6 FEET. PHOTO: TOM BROWN.

MARIAN
CLAYDEN

My early work, in the late 1960s and on into the '70s, was a systematic
exploration of traditional dyeing techniques. I was making large wall
pieces and I would take lots of time to push the techniques into new areas.

Once I decided to move into garment design, the nature of my work
changed. There are many ways to infuse depth and excitement into a
three-dimensional piece: surface treatment, color, the flair of the fabric,
draping, various trims, all add to the drama of the finished piece. There
are still elements of risk, but now it is an educated risk. When I am working with an unknown fabric, I aim for spontaneity in the early stages of
using it, but I am also watchful to see how it is affected by the dyes.
Only after this spontaneous stage do I seek a controlled, consistent result.

Sometimes I use surface techniques in a painterly way, to create an
image for contemplation. At other times, I vary the techniques to create
a mood which becomes the inspiration for a series of garments. I see
myself as a medium. Fabrics, experiences, colors, forms, images, and
time are snatched from the air. They pass through my hands and become
something magical.

Even though I create unique wearables for many known personalities,
I don't see myself in the mainstream of the industry; I am on the edge
of it. What I do is part of life's work, a continuum. The work stems from

PECTORAL, 1975; SILK; CLAMP RESIST; 84 BY 120 INCHES.

the need to communicate an idea, hopefully something that hasn't been said before. I want my work to satisfy in the same way that a good painting does. I feel that what I do is a healing thing, like a salve for our culture. This is my way of speaking in the world. I express myself with fabric and form. I want to always be reaching out—testing my fabrics, my colors, my designs, myself.

GIGANTIC HEAPS OF CRUSHED MUREX SHELLS WERE FOUND IN A 1500-1300 B.C. SITE ON THE NORTH COAST OF SYRIA. PART OF A KETTLE STAINED WITH THE PURPLE WHICH IS OBTAINED FROM THIS MOLLUSK WAS FOUND BESIDE ONE OF THESE HEAPS, AS WERE REMAINS OF DYERS' WORKSHOPS.

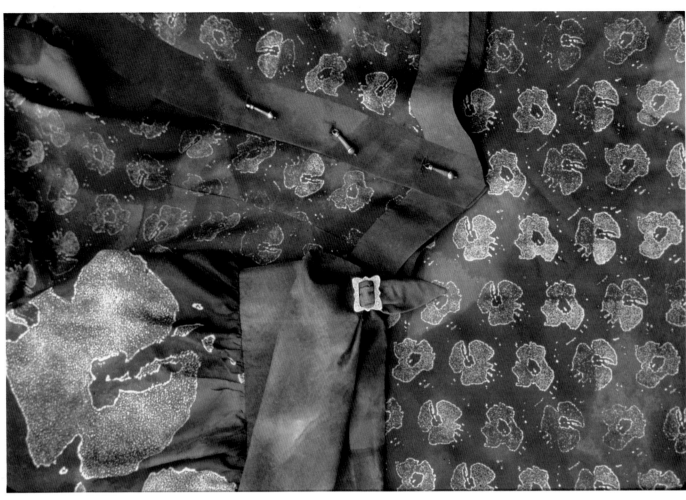

LARGE FLOWERS, SMALL FLOWERS, 1989;
SILK; SODIUM ALGENATE PRINT.

UNTITLED, 1989; SILK; SILKSCREEN PRINT, DISCHARGE DYED.

FLORENTINE DRESS, 1982; ITALIAN STRIPE SILK
CHENILLE; CLAMP RESIST.

TEXTURE AND FLEUR, 1985; COTTON CORDUROY; DOUBLE SILKSCREEN PRINT.

N A N C Y
E R I C K S O N

As I recently finished up my last oil paint diptych to tackle fabric again (after an 18-month layoff), I began wondering why I choose to work with textiles. First of all, they are incredibly versatile, but even more they are not the material of the so-called fine arts (as one curator said in my studio, "Well, this piece might be more popular with crafts, the low arts, this one, with the high arts. . ."). It is just such a division on the basis of materials or techniques that proves so perversely stimulating to me. I hope to keep blurring those distinctions through my work.

In the '60s, when I started working with fabric, I wanted to incorporate content with form and structure. I created several series: one on acid rain with large, dark quilted pieces with chemicals stitched into the fabric; another on post-nuclear disasters. **Rabbits Dancing Under Jupiter**, part of another series, is directly drawn from my experiences living with our house rabbit and the many drawings I did of him.

After a solo exhibition of all the rabbit works in the series, several people called to cite similar experiences with rabbits—watching them dance under the light of the full moon, on the crust of the first snow, on a cold, cold night. Their stories corroborated what I had simply made up by watching our rabbit "dance" around the house.

Several artists in my area started a drawing group in 1984 (still going), and

RABBITS DANCING UNDER JUPITER, 1980; COTTON, VELVET, SATIN, ACRYLICS; SEWN,
APPLIQUED, QUILTED, PAINTED; 45 BY 88 INCHES.

it was a natural transition for me at that time to introduce the human
figure into my work with all its contemporary human problems. I did a
series in which each work dealt with interior and exterior spaces in a future
world. While some calm exists in these relationships, there is also incredible conflict and disharmony.

One of the pieces, **Town on the Edge**, is also an experiment in paint
dumping. How much will the fabric take? (Some.) The title refers to the
difficulties encountered on the fringes of society, where no rules apply and
where anything can, and often does, happen. The edge-before-the-abyss
idea. I live in a beautiful place in a mountain canyon, but it's still the edge
of town. My poet friend across the road called one morning after hearing
the news and said, "A man's arm is hanging from a tree up the road. We'd
better go SEE." It was a false alarm, but real edge-of-town stuff. For
Montana, anyway.

Night of the Golden Stars is a celebration of the night. Since we don't
have too much light reflection, the stars are magnificent. When we go
down to the road on early winter mornings to get the newspaper, it's by
starlight. The lions are on a journey, just passing through, as are we all.

INHABITANTS
OF THE FIFTH-
CENTURY B.C.
CAUCASUS
REGION PAINTED
ANIMAL FIGURES
ALL OVER THEIR
CLOTHING,
PROBABLY WITH
A PASTE MADE
FROM WILD
PLANTS.

WOMAN WITH BLUE BEAR, 1992; PAPER; OIL PAINT STICKS; 26 BY 40 INCHES.

The stairs lead from one space to another, and from one world to another, and are evidence of former human habitations here on this unknown planet. In this piece, the animals, as well, have their own destiny and reality.

Although some of my works might seem as if they were done in a dream state, **Envoy** is the first time I've actually made an attempt to work with a dream. It turned out differently from the dream, as one would expect, but the sense of the lioness's waiting, and the sky and colors are like the actual dream.

For the future, I think I will continue working with similar content. In my art, the animals are acknowledged for what they are: powerful elements in life. There's a terrible poignancy in continuing to use other animals as the major focus of my work. So many of them now, in my lifetime, are becoming extinct. Their habitats and genetic pools dwindle, and human-animal conflicts increase as more land is cleared for human use everywhere. It is happening right now, all over the world. And they lose, always.

In my work animals are familiars, or spiritual guides in the lives of humans. From my standpoint, Suquamish chief Seattle said it so well: "What good is man without the beasts? If all the beasts were gone, man would die from a great loneliness of spirit."

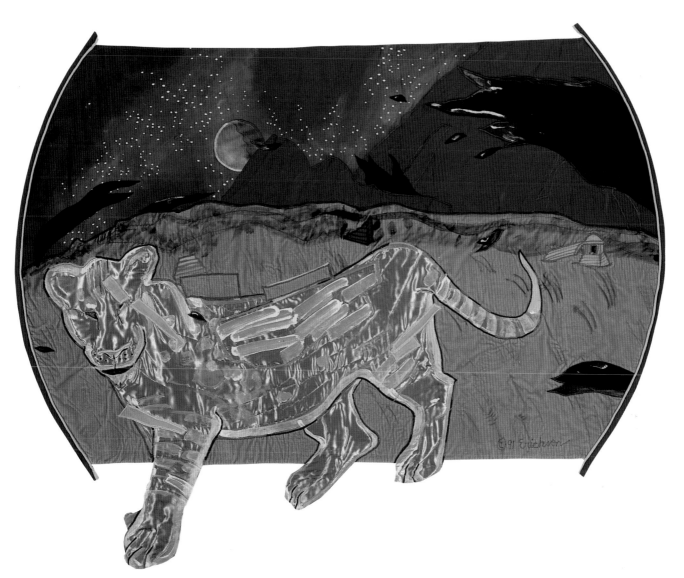

ENVOY, 1991; COTTON, VELVET, SATIN, ACRYLICS; SEWN, APPLIQUED, QUILTED, PAINTED; 51 BY 64 INCHES.

INK DRAWING FOR **ENVOY** FROM STUDIO NOTEBOOK. JOURNAL ENTRY: "DREAM A FEW NIGHTS AGO. I LOOKED OUT OF MY STUDIO & THERE SHE WAS, A GLORIOUS YELLOW-TAN AFRICAN LIONESS, LYING ON THE HILLSIDE, CLOSE. WHAT WAS SO EXTRA-ORDINARY WAS HOW ACTIVE, ALERT, NER-VOUSE(?) SHE WAS. MOVING HER HEAD, PAWS, SNAPPING—. I WENT TO THE DOORS TO BE SURE THEY WERE LOCKED."

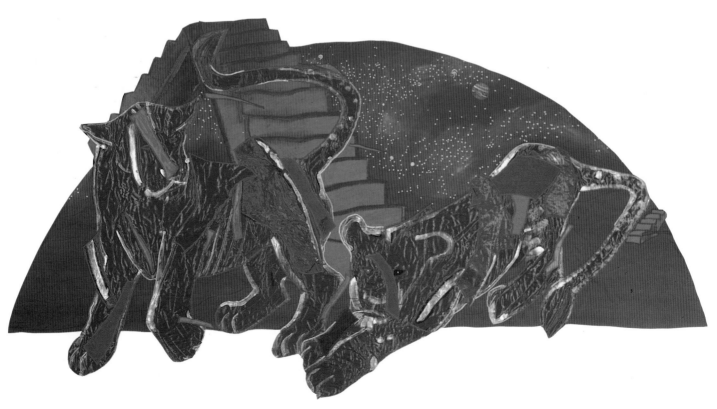

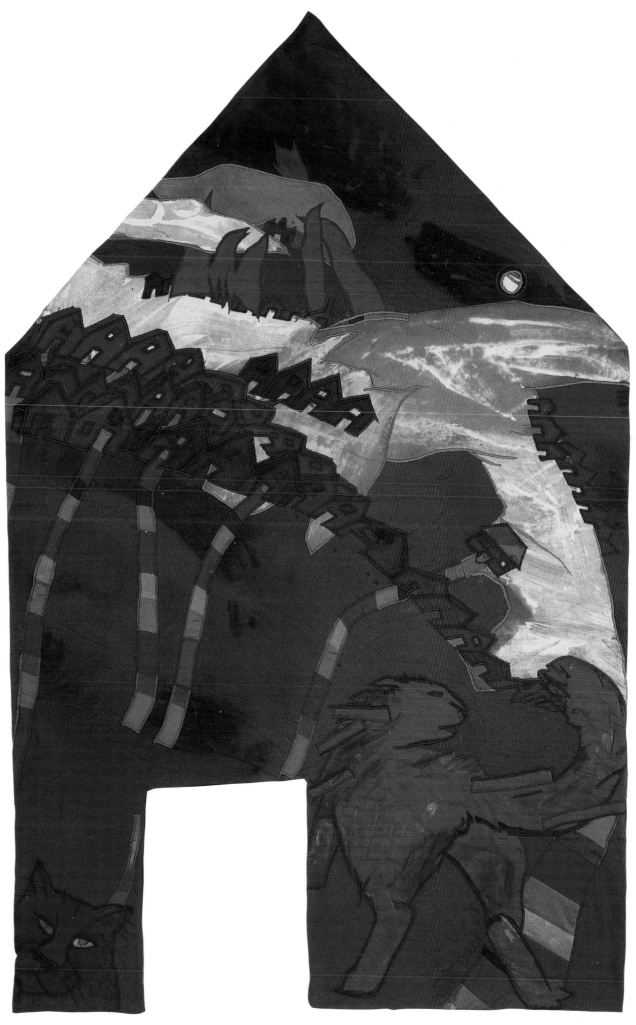

TOWN ON THE EDGE, 1986; COTTON, VELVET, SATIN, ACRYLICS; SEWN, APPLIQUED, QUILTED, PAINTED; 57 BY 37 INCHES.

JO ANN
GIORDANO

My artmaking process begins with a strong emotional reaction—to an event, a book, a work of art, or a personal experience—and a need to communicate my feelings. After deciding on a theme, I research it by reading and collecting visual images. This investigation is as satisfying to me as the physical process of creating the work. Immersed in this collection of information and images, I am faced with the challenge of distilling what is important and presenting it with subtlety, thoughtfulness, and imagination.

When I was young, my grandparents had a custom tailoring business. Trained in Italy, my grandfather prided himself on his fine craftsmanship and he was always impeccably dressed. My grandmother did all the finishing work for the men's suits. I knew that I wanted to be an artist early on, but I didn't find my chosen medium until my mid-twenties, when my interest was stimulated by a class in Japanese resist techniques. I responded enthusiastically to learning more about the textile tradition because of its emphasis on color and pattern and its connection to women's history.

Coming of age in the '60s influenced my world view and, consequently, my art. Social and political issues such as gender roles, environmental problems, and the nature of power in society are significant elements of my work. Though I am very serious about content, I feel that the use of humor makes my work more likely to increase awareness of these meaningful contemporary issues.

FAMILY PRAYER RUG, 1984; COTTON; SCREEN PRINT; 35 BY 75 INCHES.

Because of a Catholic upbringing I am imbued with a deep sense of ritual. I have vivid memories of festivals in which the statue of a saint, lavishly decorated with dollar bills and flowers, was paraded through the streets. Travel to Italy and Mexico reinforced my fascination with religious and popular art which are permeated with spiritual intensity and mystery. I want to create ritualistic objects for contemporary culture, a culture that is largely devoid of magic and ritual.

Historical textiles often serve as a springboard for ideas. My intent is to understand an object in its context and then to "make it my own," to relate it to my own experience. One such object which made a lasting impression was a Turkish talismanic robe in the Sultan Suleyman exhibit which I saw at the Metropolitan Museum of Art in New York. Designed to protect the sultan from evil, it was obsessively painted with verses from the Koran and magic number squares, all arranged in decorative patterns. I was intrigued with the way the object changed when viewed from different distances: from afar, one noticed the patterning; up close, the patterns became words and the design was revealed.

That is how I want my pieces to work. First I want to draw in the viewer with an overall impression—with the tactility of the materials, color, pattern—and then introduce an element of surprise, a "twist." Use of the decorative tradition, which is expected to be pleasing, soothing, and unprovoking, allows for a tension to be set up between expectation and reality. Andy Warhol exemplified this dynamic when he designed wallpaper using the face of Mao Tse-tung to fashion the pattern.

PERHAPS THE MOST STARTLING ANCIENT EXPERIMENTS IN FABRIC DECORATION ARE IN THE EMBROIDERY ON A GALA TUNIC OF KING TUTANKHAMON. IT HAS AN AREA JUST BELOW THE NECKLINE IN CHAIN AND RUNNING STITCHES. THE HEM OF THE GARMENT IS LAVISHLY EMBROIDERED WITH SPHINXES, GRIFFINS, AND OTHER MOTIFS, AS WELL AS THE PHARAOH'S NAME AND INSIGNIA.

Using text ties into my background as a calligrapher and graphic designer and my interest in conveying messages through my art. After overcoming my fear and resistance, I recently became computer literate. I see great potential in using the computer as a tool for designing text, pattern, and manipulating images. Experimentation is vital to my growth and development. While studying at Purdue University, I became proficient in screen printing and developed confidence in expressing my ideas. When screen printing became too restrictive, I introduced new materials and techniques, thus expanding my visual vocabulary and therefore my work.

I've learned that the surface on which I print can be expressive in itself, rather than just a neutral background. I've experimented with a variety of fabrics, spraying and resist dyeing to alter the ground fabric; I've used applique, quilting, and embroidery to achieve other surface effects. The lustrous machine embroidery on a dark wool ground in **Corporate Vestment** adds to the dimension and richness of the piece, an effect that cannot be achieved with simply screen printing. At Cranbrook Academy I began to incorporate sculptural elements into my work, using my fabric objects as part of an installation. While I feel more comfortable working two dimensionally, I will continue to explore installation work.

At midlife I reflect on the paths I have chosen for my life and my art. As I continue to evolve—as a person, an artist, a teacher—I feel that the past serves me well as a foundation, and the future beckons me with endless possibilities and opportunities.

WATER PRAYER RUG, 1992; COTTON, NETTING, SILK ORGANZA, RAYON; TIE-DYE, SCREEN PRINT, APPLIQUE, EMBROIDERY, MACHINE QUILTING; 83 BY 34 INCHES.

COPE FOR CASSANDRA, 1988; COTTON, NETTING; SCREEN PRINT, APPLIQUE; 44 BY 84 INCHES.

CORPORATE VESTMENT, 1988; SUIT COAT,
SILK; SCREEN PRINT, EMBROIDERY;
42 BY 26 BY 3 INCHES.

ROBE FOR A PROCRASTINATOR, 1991; SILK ORGANZA; SCREEN PRINT; 56 BY 48 INCHES.

TALISMANIC GARMENT II, 1988; SILK ORGANZA; SCREEN PRINT, XEROX TRANSFER; 45 BY 41 INCHES.

TALISMAN FOR FRIDA, 1990; SILK, COTTON, RAYON, HORSE HAIR, FOUND OBJECTS;
SCREEN PRINT, POLE WRAP DYE RESIST, EMBROIDERY; 41 BY 20 INCHES.

ARTURO ALONZO
SANDOVAL

In 1975 I left the loom as my major artistic tool because of the limitations
it imposed on my spontaneity. My choice to experiment with contemporary materials such as Mylar, lurex, microfilm, movie film, and computer
tape led to the ancient technique of interlacing. Because of the immediacy
of this process, I made large-scale mixed media wall pieces and sculptures.
The basic roots I learned in design and painting flourished with this simple
structural process. The structure created a surface where the natural qualities of the materials could be used as a painter uses field color and texture,
and as a surface designer uses pattern and repetition. As well, the process
produced softness of surface.

Content was dictated by the materials and structure. The **Sky Grid**
detail shows the complex nature of these early pieces and the early use of
machine stitching to achieve another addition to my oeuvre—the layering
of transparent, translucent, dense, and reflective materials to achieve more
depth and subtle texture and color variations.

The "Sky" themes led to an exploration of variations where more interior
shapes and compositional qualities were introduced. In the early 1980s,
I became fascinated with materials, using found leaded-tin tobacco barn roof-
ing, Army strap webbing, and netting to make both flat and sculptural forms.

SKY GRID, 1975, DETAIL; MYLAR, PAINT, NETTING, PLASTIC, THREAD, EYELETS; INTERLACING, STITCHING; FULL PIECE 84 BY 84 INCHES.

Using materials which were originally designed for industry was refreshing and exciting. My experiments with punched computer tape inspired me to create **Asian Poem No. 2**. In this piece, the materials of hand drawn calligraphy by Philip Cole join with the punched computer tape to form an image reminiscent of a Japanese obi or sash. The bringing together of tradition and high-tech delivers a message of modern day Japan. In developing other pieces where I used linear abstraction and form as the content, I realized that my audience for this type of work was limited.

Searching for a more symbolic format to carry messages regarding apathy of the voting populace, government control through military activism, the loss of vital programs for the poor and for education, and the corruption of government, led me to the flag of the United States as the form on which to compose. In developing the "State of the Union" series, I returned to the loom for the first six pieces. **State of the Union No. 4 (The Return of the Hostages)** was part of my first politically motivated exhibition, a show by two Vietnam veterans—myself and Jeff Durham. The impetus received from this series led to readings by Nostradamus and the Bible's Revelations.

IN LATE NEOLITHIC (3000-2500 B.C.) SPAIN, THERE WAS LITTLE CHOICE OF FIBER. ESPARTO GRASS WAS USED FOR A WIDE RANGE OF PRODUCTS: AT CUEVA DE LOS MURCIELAGOS IN ANDALUSIA, SANDALS, BASKETS, CAPS, AND EVEN FULL TUNICS WERE PRESERVED, ALL OF WHICH HAD BEEN TWINED, INTERLACED, OR WOVEN.

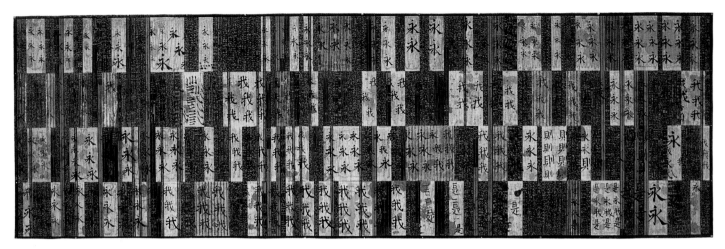

ASIAN POEM NO. 2, 1985; RICE PAPER, MICROFILM, COMPUTER PAPER, INK; CALLIGRAPHY, WATERCOLOR, INTERLACING; 44 BY 144 INCHES.

From 1965 to 1983, most of my ideas were guided by materials used, but now these same materials are the vehicle for my message. The introduction of more graphic images and language has allowed me to communicate more directly with the viewing audience. The "Ground Zero" series is where I began to employ transparent acetate copies in black and white and color to enhance the meaning of the anti-nuclear and anti-terrorist message.

In other series related to my concerns, I have tried to stress the urgency of those concerns through intense color, controlled and gestured zigzag stitches, more visible graphic images, and rigid and geometric shapes and formats. With the "Millennium" series, I am developing planetary refuges from the devastation of the earth. I envision our eyes being opened by the unveiling of yet-to-be-given information which will benefit future generations and salvage the hopes of mankind to co-exist in this vast universe. I also envision the great void of space to be filled with color and light, more beautiful than can be imagined, and I interpret eternity as a grid of interlocked time zones from which man passes easily and fluidly through space.

I wish to address serious content through beautiful materials, colors, and design. I want to leave a legacy that speaks uniquely of this time and place, and that shows it was important for me to address issues which deal with peace, hope, compassion, and passion.

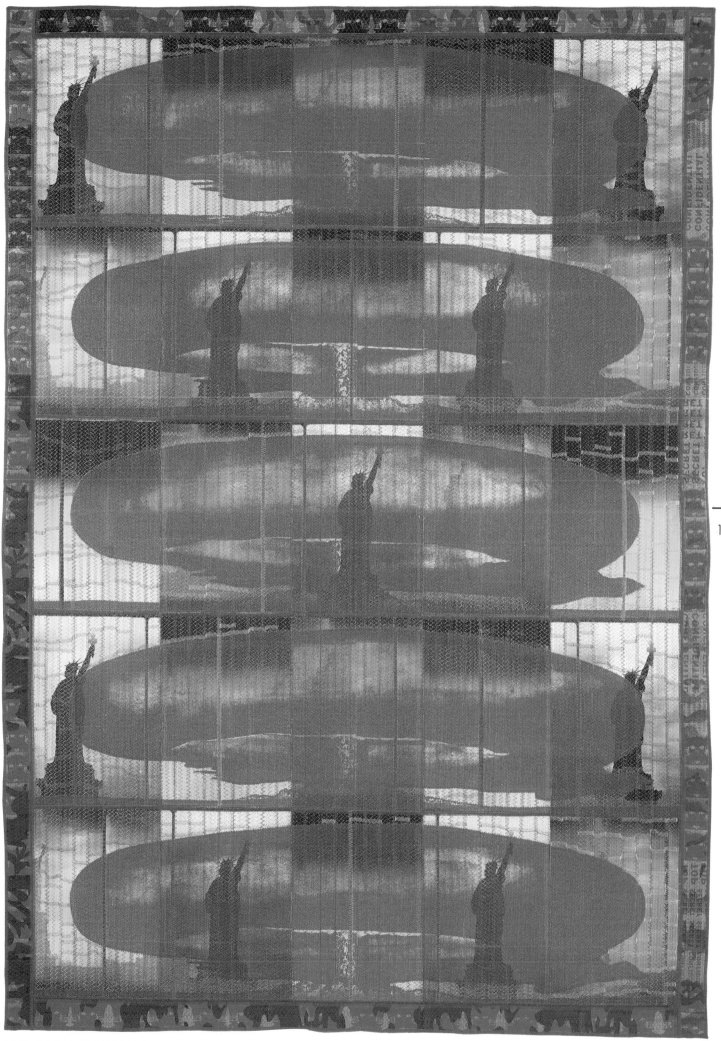

147

LADY LIBERTY/BABYLON III, 1990; ARMY STRAP WEBBING, ACETATE, NETTING, THREAD, POLYMER MEDIUM, COMMERCIAL FABRIC; MIXED MEDIA CONSTRUCTION; 87 BY 61 INCHES.

STATE OF THE UNION NO. 4 (THE RETURN OF THE HOSTAGES), 1984; COTTON, RAYON, NEWSPAPER, PLASTIC, POSTER-BOARD, POLYMER MEDIUM, INK; WOVEN COLLAGE; 40-3/4 BY 47-3/8 INCHES.

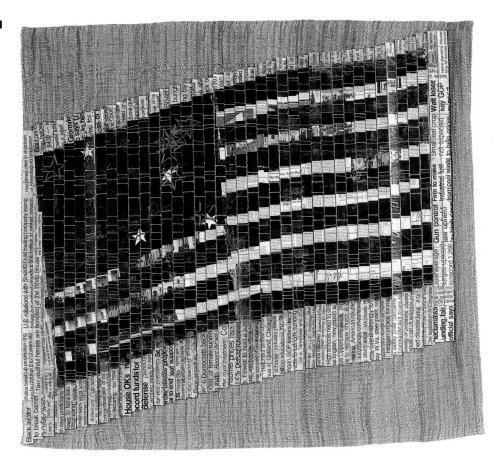

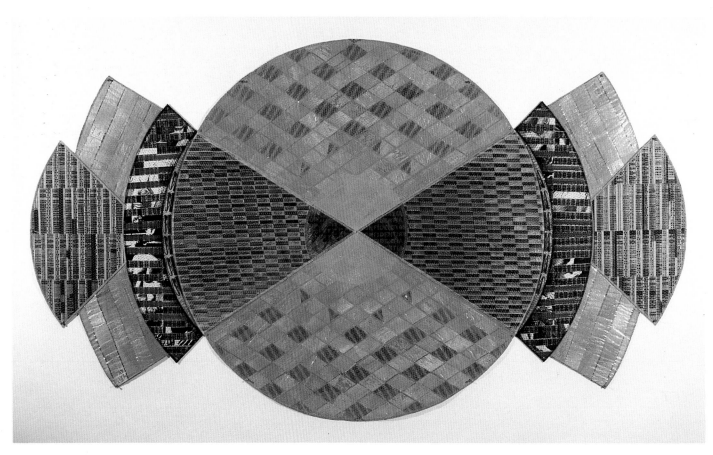

GROUND ZERO NO. 11, 1992; MYLAR, ACETATE, MICROFILM, NETTING, EYELETS; MACHINE STITCHED AND PIECED, INTERLACING, PAINTING; 54 BY 96 INCHES.

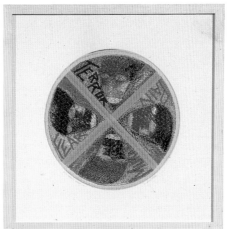

ANTI-TERRORIST BADGE NOS. 1 AND **2,**
ANTI-NUCLEAR BADGE NOS. 1 AND **2,**
1988; BLEACHED MOVIE FILM, ACETATE,
THREAD, CANVAS; PAINTING, INTERLACING,
MACHINE STITCHING; 10 BY 10 INCHES
EACH.

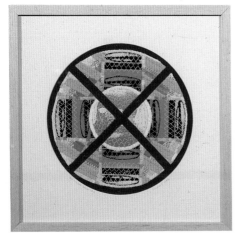

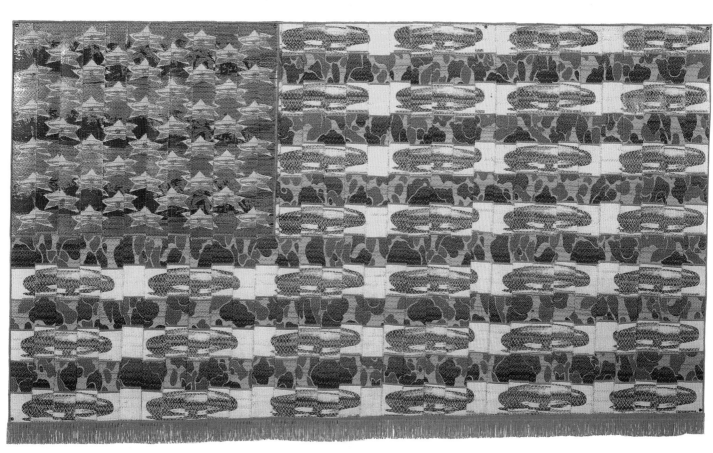

POST-NUCLEAR FLAG NO. 2, 1989; POLY/COTTON FABRIC, BRAID, RAYON, ACETATE, NETTING, MYLAR, THREAD, EYELETS; MACHINE STITCHED,
PIECED AND QUILTED, PAINTING; 36´ BY 65´ INCHES.

J A C Q U E L I N E
P E T E R S   C U L L Y

When I came to New York City in the 1950s seeking fame and fortune as a dress designer, I had no idea I would end up designing fabrics for the textile industry. I had just completed my last year of study in Paris and I was sure I would land a great job. Much to my dismay when I got to the city, I found there were no black designers or design assistants. My timing was way off. By chance, I found work as a textile colorist. Fortunately, I had a strong background in drawing, painting, and design from my years at the School of the Art Institute of Chicago.

Those first few years were fun, and I learned a lot. I had several jobs and progressed until I became a stylist, which is about as far as you can go in the field. I love working in textiles and have no regrets about not going into dress designing.

In 1978, after many years in the industry, I decided to open my own business. As the art director of the Jackie Peters Design Studio, I research the fashion market by reading trade papers and American and European fashion magazines, attending fashion shows, shopping the stores in New York City, and taking an occasional trip to Paris and Milan for firsthand information. We design directly on silk, the presentation is beautiful, and our clients respond well to this technique.

My husband is my business partner and also an artist. However, in the business he's in charge of sales. We have a dynamic working relationship

TEXTILE DESIGN, 1986; SILK; GUTTA AND WAX DYE RESIST. PHOTO COURTESY THE ARTIST.

and complement each other very well. Being an African American in the garment center has not presented too many problems, but being a woman has been a problem. On the business end, I deal mostly with men and it is sometimes difficult to get their attention and respect. Enter my husband. If they won't listen to me, they will listen to him. There has been some improvement in this area over the years, but it is slow going.

The firm represents eight to ten freelance artists whom I meet with every Tuesday to review their designs. Our sessions are a lot like critiques and we all learn from the process. The artists find it a good way of working because they are not working in a vacuum. I give each designer several assignments weekly, keeping in mind the strengths of each one; that is to say, some designers are better in certain areas than others. The next week, they bring in the refined designs, we process and catalog them. We design primarily for women's apparel, but sometimes these designs find their way into men's wear and home furnishings. I'm very fortunate to work in a field that excites me and in which I look forward to going to work.

Since 1983 I've been doing watercolors on paper. When I was asked to be a presenter and exhibitor at the 1992 Southeast Surface Design

A HALF DOZEN PURE SILK OBJECTS WERE RECOVERED FROM A FIFTH-CENTURY SITE IN ATHENS, GREECE. THE PURPLE AND WHITE SILKS WERE PROBABLY EXPENSIVE LUXURIES SINCE THEY WERE VERY LIKELY IMPORTED FROM THE EAST.

symposium, I decided to try my hand at painting on silk. I focus on images that express my heritage, painting musicians, family members, African weavers, masks, and symbols.

The whole process is fascinating and allows me a spontaneity that is stimulating. I don't have to think about the colors I am using or whether the technique is printable. I have complete freedom of expression. When I am doing fabric design, I keep in mind the current trends, colors, and product—that is, whether it is for a dress, blouse, swimsuit, etc. When I am painting, I can let myself go and hope that my message will reach someone out there. In either case, whether I create a good design or a good painting, I feel a sense of accomplishment and joy.

COTTON SPINNER, 1992; SILK; GUTTA DYE RESIST; 20 BY 16 INCHES. PHOTO: LISA HERMANSON.

TEXTILE DESIGN, 1986; SILK; GUTTA DYE RESIST.

VISIONS OF THE SPIRIT, 1992; SILK; GUTTA DYE RESIST AND DIRECT DYE; 16-1/2 BY 33-1/2 INCHES. PHOTO: LISA HERMANSON.

LEE
BALE

The work comes out of an interest in pattern as a contemporary visual language, much as pattern has always been a rich form of decoration, sign, and symbol historically. There is also an acknowledgement to the heritage of pattern as textile. Patterns emerge from the urban matrix: many-layered city walls and grid forms. I want to achieve the feeling of density and compressed, suffocating space, but with an underlying electric current of vital human energy.

The dresses also come from the city, but as remnants, cast-offs, and recycled objects. I want them to have character, posture, animation, to dance. The format ultimately represents person or personage and allows me to respond on an intimate level to relationships. Often the garment becomes a symbol of self. Architecture is the others, the world, the place of dwelling. My work is not really about these objects; rather, what is around these objects.

Garment as a symbol functions in a dual role. One is the bearer of messages about society and the times. It does this largely through ornament and decoration. Another role is the sculptural form of dress. Paring away the design and structure and reducing a garment to its simplest shape reveals an essence of shelter that might be, alternately, heaven or hell. Garment is imbued with the power of protector, enabler, definer. (Consider the dress as vessel. The dress by itself is, of course, understood

LIGHT AT THE END, 1980; XEROX PAPER; SCREEN PRINT COLLAGE; 82 BY 45 INCHES.

to be empty. No matter how rich or lavish the shell of the fabric vessel, it is its emptiness that permits entry, or the alternative possibility of fullness that informs.)

The act of coming to the work must be one of sifting through shifting layers to find what lies beneath. I think of a junk shop—just layers and layers of stuff. This is a peculiarly American neurosis, I think, this fascination for saving and accumulating. There is an unfinished quality in this "gathering" relationship between people and things. You can see it around the edges—the do-it-yourself project that never gets done, the rough edges in people's lives. My dress prints are many-layered. Images are held in tension between layers of overprinted grids and patterns.

In recent pieces, the dress as a figurative vehicle gave way to the representation of the human figure itself. As always, the method of working and the materials are chosen to evoke my conscious desire to articulate self at the edge, the hem of things. The bare bones of crinoline evoke enclosure. I made a series of drawings with a garment form that attempted to summon the memory of what it felt like to wear a crinoline, especially the prickly place where the zipper stopped. I would draw a dress turned inside-out, revealing all the seam edges, and cover it with brittle shellac or flock pink dryer lint on a tissue paper shirt shape. These early studies produced the "washed drawings." I work a drawn canvas surface heavily with

A NUMBER OF TEXTILES WERE FOUND IN THE BOTTOM OF A SIXTH CENTURY B.C. SALT MINE IN GERMANY. THE HALLSTAT ARTISANS WHO MADE THEM HAD A PENCHANT FOR COMBINING A VARIETY OF TECHNIQUES IN ONE PIECE. IN SHREDS, THEY WERE STILL FINE EXAMPLES. A RAG WRAPPED AROUND AN AXE HANDLE HAD STRIPES ON ITS EDGE AND A DESIGN OF CHANGING CHECKER PATTERNS ALONGSIDE.

charcoal and stitching and various kinds of marking, tearing, and abrasion. After washing, the figures shrink and wrinkle and the cloth seems to age and develop a skin-like quality. The figure in my work is often an imaginary generic "human" that I refer to as "the poet"—an everyman or every woman representation.

For the installation, **Holding On/Up: 12 Yards of Body Parts**, I worked nose to table crawling around on a printing table, drawing about 30 studies of my own body that I could render as details. I wanted to examine the parts of my body that caused discomfort or awkwardness, both physical and emotional. And I wanted to explore the relationship between pain and what was painful. Many of the vignettes evolved into representations that are submerged into a riotous, carnival print of patterns, grids, and colors.

In choosing fabric as an arena, I was lured by the tactility of cloth and how its visceral nature evokes a strong correlation to the physical body. Also, it is humble, domestic, marginalized even—an opposite position from the elitist, hierarchical, modernist art that I was trained in. Rather than the philosophical intellectualizing of the art process, I longed for pure sensation. I want to make and provoke a gut response through visual work.

156

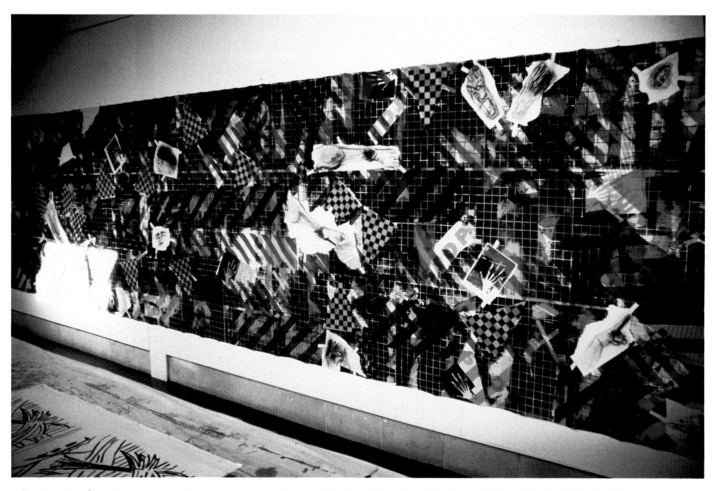

HOLDING ON/UP: 12 YARDS OF BODY PARTS, 1991; SCREEN PRINT AND CHARCOAL ON CANVAS; 72 INCHES BY 12 YARDS.

HOLDING ON/UP, DETAIL.

TAXI DANCE, 1986; SCREEN PRINT, COLLAGE; 60 BY 60 INCHES.

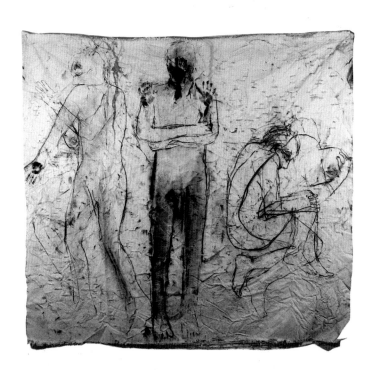

UNTITLED "WASHED DRAWING," 1989; CHARCOAL ON CANVAS; 96 BY 96 INCHES.

MARY ANNE
JORDAN

Patterns have travelled through history, often being transformed during
their migration. This evolution of pattern is especially evident within the
textile medium, since fabrics have carried patterns embedded in their structures and applied to their surfaces for thousands of years. A pattern may
have originated as a symbol or structural element but eventually became
a decoration or an embellishment.

Through an extended history, a pattern (and the swatch of fabric that
carries it) becomes layered with meanings and associations; the references
are potentially historical, cultural, and political as well as visual.

Many different textile traditions, especially the innumerable ways these
traditions have used pattern, have influenced and inspired my work.
A few of the sources that I have looked at closely include 19th- and
20th-century American quilts, Kuba (Zaire) applique skirts and raffia
velvets, and Japanese shibori fabrics.

Traditions of other media, past and present, as well as the products of
popular culture, are resources for information and ideas: Haitian metal-
work and voodoo banners; Japanese screen paintings of the Edo Period;
pop painting of the 1960s; printed advertisements and post cards.

My work is a series of reactions to my study of patterns, history, and
my own everyday experiences. I juxtapose and superimpose seemingly

WHEATS & LADDERS, 1987; COTTON; SCREEN PRINT, BLEACHOUT, APPLIQUE; 96 BY 144 INCHES.

unrelated patterns and fabrics using a variety of techniques. I screen print, paint, and dye fabrics, which are then pieced and overlaid together. After the initial construction, I continue to print, paint, applique, and stitch on the surface. It is a building process that connects and contrasts fabrics, patterns, and images.

Informed by the kinds of resources I have listed, my intention is not to recreate the resource; I hope to convey some of the same energy, tension, and/or excitement I have drawn from them. I am interested in the marriage of contrasting imagery and the irony that results in the offspring of unlikely combinations. It is in these combinations of ideas, patterns, and fabrics that I find my impetus to work. New images and ideas built through the working process teach me to look at the world with new eyes.

A SPECTACULAR GROUPING OF FABRIC WAS FOUND IN FIFTH-CENTURY B.C. GRAVE MOUNDS IN THE ALTAI MOUNTAINS BY RUSSIAN ARCHAEOLOGISTS. SHAWLS, RUGS, HORSE BLANKETS, AND A TENT WERE ALL DECORATED BY THE APPLIQUE METHOD OF SEWING SHAPED CLOTH TO CLOTH OF ANOTHER COLOR.

WEDDING RINGS & BABY BLOCKS, 1990; COTTON; SCREEN PRINT, DIRECT APPLICATION OF DYE, APPLIQUE, EMBROIDERY; 48 BY 48 INCHES.

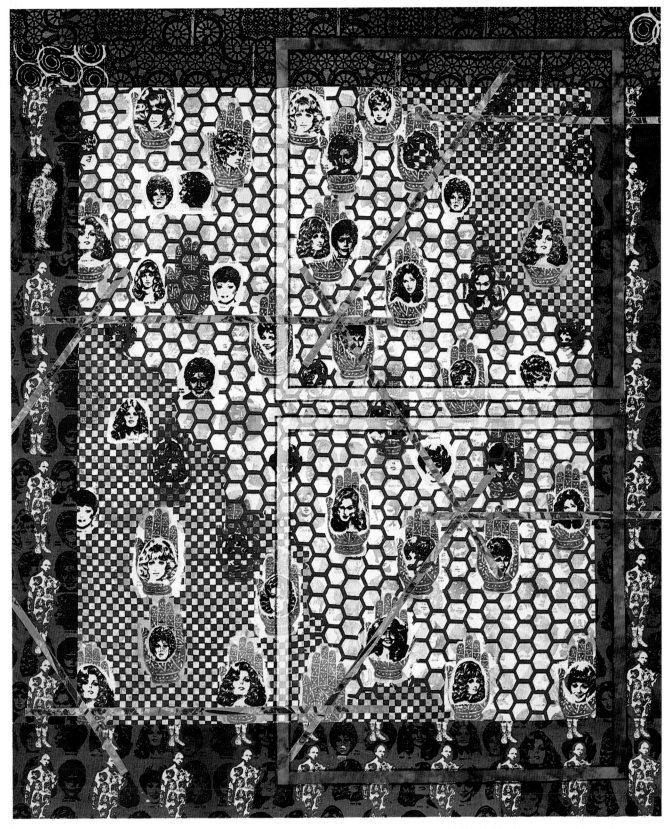

BETWEEN THE LINES, 1990; COTTON; SCREEN PRINT, STITCHED, APPLIQUE, EMBROIDERY; 48 BY 72 INCHES.

TATTOOED LADIES, 1991; COTTON; SCREEN PRINT, VAT DYED, APPLIQUE, EMBROIDERY;
48 BY 48 INCHES.

DREAMS, 1991; COMMERCIAL FABRIC; SCREEN PRINT, DIRECT APPLICATION OF DYE,
STITCHED, APPLIQUE, EMBROIDERY; 48 BY 48 INCHES.

CROSS MY PALM, 1991; COTTON; SCREEN PRINT, DIRECT APPLICATION OF DYE, APPLIQUE, BLEACHOUT; 48 BY 48 INCHES.

When I graduated from college with a print major in 1987, my interest was in designing fabric for the fashion industry. My designs were used for hats, coats, shirts, and jackets. Later I designed for home furnishings. This work included painted and printed floor cloths, cushions, upholstery, and drapery fabric.

As I worked on production pieces though, I kept feeling myself being pulled in another direction. I began to print large banners that were inspired by images and signage from the Queen Street and Kensington Market areas in Toronto. Kensington Market is a vibrant, multi-cultural marketplace in downtown, and is one of Toronto's landmarks. Queen Street is the artists' ghetto. The banners depicting this area have graffiti and decorative markings, which are a takeoff of the spray painted, stencilled, and hand painted images I saw on walls and doors in the alleyways there.

The banners were a major divergence because they were my first pieces that combined imagery with storytelling. My previous work dealt with mark making and repeat pattern.

While I was researching the Portuguese district in Toronto, I discovered a statue. Drawn to its classical beauty, I jumped the fence and photographed it. Initially what excited me was simply the idea of printing fabric with this

classical image of a woman. Over time, what unfolded on cloth was the story of a female statue raised in the backyard of a downtown Toronto dwelling.

In my imagination, the statue is a mythological goddess who has been reborn into modern time. She is larger than life. Her physique is made of stone. To me, this material reflects the history of women—fixed into position, without mobility or flexibility, whose identities were made at birth and who were little more than property.

Exploration of the statue evolved into a series of ongoing collages that became the forum for my investigation of the image and what it evoked within me. It wasn't until I titled the first pieces that I realized I was telling a story. In 1990 I was invited to be an artist in residence at The Banff Centre for the Arts in Alberta. When I arrived, I thought I was

IT IS NOT UNUSUAL FOR THE HISTORY OF A CLAN OR SOCIAL GROUP TO BE CAREFULLY RECORDED IN A SERIES OF IMAGES, EACH OF WHICH ENCAPSULATES THE MOST IMPORTANT EVENT OF A PERIOD OF TIME.

THE RESOLVE, 1991; COTTON; SCREEN PRINT, PAINTING; 84 BY 30-1/2 INCHES. PHOTO: JEREMY JONES.

going to put the statue series to rest. When I left after making six more pieces, I realized, to my surprise and delight, that the series was alive and "to be continued."

In the process of image manipulation, I use multiple screen printing and photo emulsion/photographic imagery, combined with stencilling and hand painting. This way of working lends itself to a progression of images. I use color to convey a mood or feeling.

I print because I love the physicality of the medium. The printing process suits my personality and creative energy. Through this technique, I have discovered, and given myself, unlimited freedom in how I can approach cloth and apply my ideas.

ON HER THIRTIETH BIRTHDAY SHE SIGNED A CONTRACT WITH STATUESQUE PERFUMI
1989; COTTON; SCREEN PRINT, PAINTING; 23-1/4 BY 14 INCHES. PHOTO: JEREMY JONES.

LEE BALE, 11206-117 St., Edmonton, Alb., Canada T5G 2W2

Lee Bale received an M.F.A. from Cranbrook Academy of Art and has taught at the School of the Art Institute of Chicago, University of California-Davis Department of Environmental Design, Kent (Ohio) State University School of Art, and the University of Wisconsin-Milwaukee. She has given workshops and lectures, and has been a set designer, sign design consultant, textile conservation assistant, printer, and an installation assistant. Her work has been exhibited in "An Urban Matrix," "Dynamic Dimensions," "About Fiber," "Baked Alaska," and "Natural Influence: A National Textile Review."

BETSY STERLING BENJAMIN, 419 Yabunoshita-cho Tonodan, Kamikyo-ku, Kyoto, 602 Japan

Since 1990, Betsy Sterling Benjamin has been a lecturer for Doshisha University, Kyoto and at Kyoto Sangyo University since 1989. She has had solo shows in Hiroshima, Tokyo, and Kyoto, Japan and in Paradise Valley, Arizona. Other exhibits include "Three Artists, Three Countries, Three Ways" (Kyoto), "Art to Wear '84" (Pittsburgh, Pennsylvania), "Celebration" (Kyoto), and "Art Crossing" (Kyoto). Her work is held in several corporate collections and has been published in *FIBERARTS*, *Surface Design Journal*, and *School Arts Magazine*.

D'ARCIE BEYTEBIERE, 2157 - 7th West, Seattle, WA 98119

D'Arcie Beytebiere received an M.F.A. in Textile Design from the University of Washington in Seattle and, in 1992, an Arts Education Fellowship from the Council for Basic Education/National Endowment for the Arts. Her work was exhibited in "Northwest Designer Craftsmen," "Wearable Art," and the 1992 faculty exhibition at Arrowmont School of Arts and Crafts, Gatlinburg, Tennessee. She has been an instructor on shibori techniques at Arizona State University, Alaska Weaver's Co-op, national conferences of the Surface Design Association, and a number of other places throughout the United States. Beytebiere is an art instructor in the Edmonds (Washington) School District.

MARNA GOLDSTEIN BRAUNER, 2907 E. Hampshire, Milwaukee, WI 53211

Marna Goldstein Brauner has been associate professor of art at the University of Wisconsin-Milwaukee since 1989. She has an M.F.A. in Textiles from the California College of Arts and Crafts. In 1991, she received the Milwaukee County individual artist's fellowship award, and in 1992, the Wisconsin Arts Board individual artist new work award. Selected invitational exhibits are "Pictorial Space: New Images in Textiles," "The Fabric of Life: Contemporary American Works in Fiber," "Perspectives from the Rim," "Celebrating the Stitch" (traveling through 1994), and "Domestic Ontogeny: New Textile Forms." Her work was published in *Ontario Craft Magazine, FIBERARTS, Textilforum, Celebrating the Stitch*, and *Fiberarts Design Book Four*. Brauner has lectured extensively and was a visiting artist at Nova Scotia College of Art and Design, School of the Art Institute of Chicago, Sheridan College in Ontario, and the Textile Art Centre in Chicago.

DOROTHY CALDWELL, 201 Front St. E., Hastings, Ont., Canada KOL IYO

A founding member of Surfacing: Textile Dyers' and Printers' Association of Canada, Dorothy Caldwell was the 1990 recipient of the Bronfman Award. She has exhibited widely in Canada, in both group and solo shows. Her work was accepted into the International Shibori Exhibition 1992 shown in Nagoya, Japan. Caldwell's work is in many collections, including Ontario Crafts Council, Canadian Crafts Council, and the Canadian Museum of Civilization, which produced the video "Dorothy Caldwell" in 1991.

NICK CAVE, 1347 S. Michigan Ave., Chicago, IL 60605

Nick Cave had a Ford Foundation scholarship to attend Cranbrook Academy of Art, from which he received his M.F.A. in 1989. He is fulltime visiting artist at the School of the Art Institute of Chicago. Group exhibitions include "Fashion as Art," "Young Americans," "Rites of Spring," and "From Cultures Beyond." In 1988, he sat for photographers Steven Arnold and Robert Mapplethorpe. He began performing in 1987, opening that year for Karen Finley at Cranbrook. Articles on Cave's performance work were published in *Exeter* and *FIBERARTS*.

MARIAN CLAYDEN, 101 Church St., Los Gatos, CA 95032

Marian Clayden has work in the permanent collections of the Victoria & Albert Museum, London, American Crafts Museum and Cooper-Hewitt Museum, New York, and Dromes Museum in France. Among invitational shows her work has appeared in since 1974 are "Dyers Art" (Museum of Contemporary Crafts, New York), "Fiberworks America and Japan" (Museum of Modern Art, Kyoto), "The Fiber Art Mainstream" (Museum of Modern Art, San Francisco), "Surface Design" (Dromes Museum, France), "Color, Light & Surface" (Cooper-Hewitt Museum, New York), and "Extravagant Lengths in Velvet" (FIT Gallery, New York). Her fabrics were used to design costumes for the musical, *Hair*. In 1981 she set up the fashion design house, Clayden.

JACQUELINE PETERS CULLY, 6 Meroke Ct., Huntington Station, NY 11746

In 1978 Jacqueline Peters Cully started Jackie Peters Design Studio in New York City. She studied at Chambre Syndicale De L'Ecole Couture Parisenne in Paris, School of the Art Institute at Chicago, and Parsons School of Design, where she taught for nine years. She has had solo shows at Christina Cultural Arts Center, Wilmington, Delaware, Gallery of the Unitarian Church, and the Huntington Arts Council, Huntington, New York. Culy is represented by Gallery Madison 90 and Ward Nasse Gallery of New York City, Spiral Gallery, Dorsey's Gallery, and Asssociation of Caribbean-American Artists Gallery in Brooklyn, and the Primavera Gallery in Huntington.

LENORE DAVIS, P.O. Box 47, Newport, KY 41072

Lenore Davis has been a self-employed studio artist and workshop teacher since 1969. She has exhibited her soft sculpture and two-dimensional work throughout the United States, including shows at Wheeler-Seidel Gallery, New York City, Kentucky Art & Craft Foundation, Louisville, Washington Square, Washington, D.C., Contemporary Arts Gallery, Portland, Oregon, Hunter Museum of Art, Chattanooga, Tennessee, and Midland Center for the Arts, Midland, Michigan. She is a member of Surface Design Association, American Craft Council, and Friends of Fiber Art International.

NANCY N. ERICKSON, 3250 Pattee Canyon Rd., Missoula, MT 59803

Nancy Erickson holds an M.F.A. in painting from the University of Montana. Her work was included in *Celebrating the Stitch* and *Fiberarts Design Books Three* and *Four*. She has shown her work in many group, juried, and invitational exhibits, including "Human Shelter" (New York City), "Surface and Structure: Concepts in Fiber" (Vashon, Washington), "Contemporary Quilts: Spirit of the Nineties" (Kalamazoo, Michigan), "Contemporary Voices from the Plains" (Ames, Iowa), and "A Celebration of Red" (San Jose, California). Erickson recently had solo shows at Sutton West Gallery in Missoula and the Montana Gallery in Arlington, Virginia.

DEBORAH J. FELIX, 1029 Grayson St., Berkeley, CA 94710

Deborah Felix has taught at Berkeley High School, in the Fiber Department at California State University at Northridge, and in the Textile Department at Saddleback Community College in Mission Viejo, California. She has a long list of exhibitions, including "Small Works" (Mobilia Gallery, Boston), "Tea x 2" (Faith Nightengale Gallery, San Diego, California), "The Art of Narrating" (New Pieces Gallery, Berkeley, California), "Beyond Boundaries" (Gallery 53, Cooperstown, New York), and "Quilt National '91" at the Dairy Barn, Athens, Ohio. In 1992 her work was published in the *Surface Design Journal* and *FIBERARTS* magazine.

JO ANN GIORDANO, 13542 Cedar Rd., University Heights, OH 44118

Jo Ann Giordano studied at Rhode Island School of Design, Purdue University, and received an M.F.A. from Cranbrook Academy of Art in 1988. Selected exhibits since 1981 include "Ceremonial Garments" (High Point, North Carolina), "Artforms" (Lafayette, Indiana), "Fiber: The Next Generation" (Normal, Illinois), "Face to Face: Cranbrook/Mexico" (Bloomfield Hills, Michigan), "Focus: Fiber" (Cleveland, Ohio), "Threads" (Piermont, New York), "New Ends" (Staten Island, New York), and "Form and Object: Contemporary Interpretations of Craft Traditions" (Laramie, Wyoming). She is an instructor in fiber arts at Kent State University School of Art.

ANA LISA HEDSTROM, 1420 - 45th St., Emeryville, CA 94608

Ana Lisa Hedstrom's wearables are represented by Obiko (San Francisco and New York), Julie: Artisans Gallery, New York, The Hand and the Spirit Gallery, Scottsdale, Arizona, and Wittenborn-Hollingsworth, Los Angeles, California. She studied at Kyoto Art College in Japan and Mills College in Oakland, California. Her work has been published in *Shibori: The Inventive Art of Japanese Shaped Resist Dyeing, Art to Wear, California Designers*, and a number of magazines. Her work is in the permanent collection of The Smithsonian Institution's Cooper-Hewitt Museum, Takeda Kahei Shoten in Arimatsu, Japan, and Aichi Shibori Research and Study Archive, Nagoya, Japan.

MARY ANNE JORDAN, U. of Kansas, School of Fine Arts, Room 300-Art & Design, Lawrence, KS 66045

Mary Anne Jordan has been in the design department at the University of Kansas since 1986. She received her M.F.A. from Cranbrook Academy of Art in 1985. Selected exhibits include "Anniversary Show" at Textile Arts International, Minneapolis, Minnesota, "Fiber: The Next Generation," Illinois State University, Normal, "Fiber Structure National VI" at the Downey (California) Museum of Art, "Somewhere I Have Never Travelled," Appalachian Center for Crafts in Smithville, Tennessee, "Contemporary Fiber," Saint Mary's College, Notre Dame, Indiana, "Twenty American Textile Artists," U.S. Embassy in Warsaw, Poland, and "Seeing Through Layers" at the Museum for Textiles in Toronto, Ontario.

GLEN KAUFMAN, University of Georgia, Department of Art, Athens, GA 30602

Since 1962 Glen Kaufman has exhibited in too many group shows to list. He has had almost forty solo shows, the most recent being "Reflections—East and West" at the Azabu Museum of Arts and Crafts in Tokyo, Japan and the Lamar Dodd Art Center in LaGrange, Georgia. He is a recipient of a Fulbright Grant, Ford Foundation Grant, two faculty research grants from the University of Georgia, and several grants from the National Endowment for the Arts. Kaufman is an honorary life member of the Surface Design Association, a fellow of the American Craft Council, and a Phi Beta Delta member of the Honor Society for International Scholars. He also is a member of the American Craft Council and World Craft Council. He is professor in charge of fabric design, professor of art, and on the graduate faculty of the University of Georgia.

DEBORAH KIRKEGAARD, c/o Page Active Design, 9 Tecumseth St., Toronto, Ont. M5V 3G4, Canada

Deborah Kirkegaard has exhibited in a number of group shows throughout Canada. She had a solo show at the centre des arts visuels, Montreal, in 1991. She has been a display designer, art director, and a teacher. She was the recipient of a three year residency from Harbourfront Textile Studio, Toronto, and the 1991 M. Joan Chalmers Award for Fibre from the Ontario Crafts Council.

ANNE M. LINDBERG, 5117 Wyandotte #3N, Kansas City, MO 64112

Anne Lindberg is a fulltime instructor in the Foundations Department of Kansas City Art Institute. She holds an M.F.A. from Cranbrook Academy of Art. She has exhibited in many group shows, including "Dyeing to Resist," Textile Arts International, Minneapolis, "Paper/Fiber XIII," Iowa City, "International Fiberart '91," Pittsburgh Center for the Arts, and "KCAI Fellows." In 1992, Lindberg did a collaborative installation with Piper Shepard at Dolphin in Kansas City, a three-person show at Carleton College, Northfield, Minnesota, and showed work at the International Shibori Symposium in Nagoya, Japan. She was the 1992 recipient of a faculty development grant and a departmental travel grant from the Kansas City Art Institute.

ANNE MCKENZIE NICKOLSON, 5020 N. Illinois St., Indianapolis, IN 46208

Anne McKenzie Nickolson earned her M.F.A. in Textile Design from Indiana University. She received an artist in residence fellowship from Artpark in Lewiston, New York and a technical assistance grant from the Arts Council of Indianapolis. Selected shows in which her work has been exhibited are "Threads: Seven American Artists and Their Miniature Textile Pictures" (The Renwick Gallery), "New Artists: New Approaches" (Gayle Wilson Gallery), "Pictorial and Narrative Fibers" (traveling), "Fiberart International 1991" (Pittsburgh Center for the Arts), "Homage to Diane Itter" (Helen Drutt Gallery, Philadelphia), and "Celebrating the Stitch" (traveling through 1994).

MICHAEL OLSZEWSKI, 703 Carpenter Lane, Philadelphia, PA 19119

Since 1982 Michael Olszewski has been chair of the Textile Department at Moore College of Art and Design in Philadelphia. He received his M.F.A. from Cranbrook Academy of Art in 1977 and a National Endowment for the Arts Fellowship in 1979. He has shown in a number of group shows including "Contemporary Fabric Design" at the University of Delaware, "Works in Fibers" at Tyler School of Art, "Poetry of the Physical" at the American Craft Museum, "Fiber Art" at Drexel University, Philadelphia, "Perspectives from the Rim" at Bellevue (Washington) Art Museum, and "Fiber Art" at Maveety Gallery in Salishan, Oregon. Olszewski has had solo shows at Nexus Gallery and Helen Drutt Gallery in Philadelphia, and Eve Mannes Gallery in Atlanta.

JUNCO SATO POLLACK, 11 Polo Dr., N.E., Atlanta, GA 30309

Junco Sato Pollack has exhibited widely throughout Japan and the United States. She was in the 1988 Salon International de L'Ameublement in Monza, Italy, and has shown recently in the "Contemporary Art and Silk" exhibit at the Textile Museum in Terassa, Spain and the Musee Historique Des Tissus in Lyon, France. Her work has been published in *American Craft, Surface Design Journal,* and *FIBERARTS.* She has lectured extensively and taught workshops on textile design, decorative arts, weaving, and shibori. Pollack received an M.F.A. in Textile Design from Rochester (New York) Institute of Technology in 1991 and is assistant professor at the School of Art and Design, Georgia State University in Atlanta.

JASON POLLEN, 4348 Locust St., Kansas City, MO 64110

In 1992, Jason Pollen received the Idea Como Award for Most Exceptional Printed and Dyed Fabric, Como, Italy. In 1991, he was a first-place winner of the Japan Fashion Foundation textile design contest and received a Mid America Arts Alliance/National Endowment for the Arts fellowship. Selected group exhibitions include "The Dyer's Art" (Pacific Design Center, Los Angeles), "Adornments" (Bernice Steinbaum Gallery, New York), "New Directions in Fiber" (Interwoven Designs Gallery, St. Louis), "American Craft at the Armory" (New York), "Perspectives from the Rim" (Bellevue Museum, Seattle), and "Natural Influence: A National Textile Review" (Rochester Institute of Technology). Pollen has been a textile designer for Jack Lenor Laren, Perry Ellis, Oscar de la Renta, Yves St. Laurent, Jantzen Swimwear, and Nieman-Marcus. He is currently in the Fiber Department at the Kansas City Art Institute.

VICTORIA Z. RIVERS, 2131 - 51st St., Sacramento, CA 95817

Since 1978 Victoria Rivers has shown her work in more than a hundred group exhibits. Recent invitational shows are "Abstraction" and "Mixed Bag Invitational" (Sacramento City College, California), "Connected Through Fiber" (Santa Rosa Junior College, California), "Creative Energy: An Exhibit of Neon Art" (City of Brea Gallery, California), and "Natural Influence: A National Textile Review" (Rochester Institute of Technology, New York). Rivers has lectured extensively in North America, and in 1990, to four national institutions in India, including The American Center at Bombay and the National Institute of Design in Gujarat. She was the 1990-91 recipient of an Indo-American Fellowship from the Council for the International Exchange of Scholars. Rivers spent the winter of 1992 in India doing research on traditional light-reflective textiles for a forthcoming book. She is professor of textiles at the University of California-Davis.

ARTURO ALONZO SANDOVAL, P.O. Box 237, Lexington, KY 40584

Arturo Alonzo Sandoval is a tenured professor in the Art Department at the University of Kentucky, Lexington. He earned his M.F.A. from Cranbrook Academy of Art. He has lectured and presented workshops throughout the United States and presented a slide lecture, "Current Political Art Forms: A Personal View," during the 14th International Biennial of Tapestry in Lausanne, Switzerland. He has juried many competitions, including the 1990 Piccolo Spoleto Craft Festival, "Kentucky Contemporary '90," and "BASF Fiber Arts '91." His work has been exhibited in a long list of regional, national and international shows, and is in many museum and corporate collections. Sandoval was awarded a 1992 Visual Arts Fellowship from the National Endowment for the Arts.

JACQUELINE TRELOAR, 100 Dowling Ave., Toronto, Ont., Canada M6K 3A4

Jacqueline Treloar has had solo shows at The Carnegie Gallery, the Ontario Crafts Council, and the Homer Watson Gallery in Ontario. She has been a colorist for fashion and home furnishings designers, a buyer and wardrobe assistant for movies, and done costumes for the Stratford Festival, Charlottetown Festival, and National Ballet of Canada. Treloar was a 1990/91 recipient of an Ontario Arts Council exhibitions assistance grant.

CLARE M. VERSTEGEN, School of Art, Arizona State University, Tempe, AZ 85287-1505

In addition to being assistant professor in the School of Art at Arizona State University, Clare Verstegen teaches and lectures throughout the United States. She has been an instructor at Arrowmont School of Arts and Crafts in Gatlinburg, Tennessee since 1989, and taught at Penland (North Carolina) School of Crafts in 1992 and 1993. She was a 1992 visiting artist at Savannah (Georgia) College of Art and Design and will be an instructor at the 1994 Quilt/Surface Design Symposium in Columbus, Ohio. She holds an M.F.A. from Cranbrook Academy of Art. Verstegen has juried several shows, most recent being the national "Pattern: New Form/New Function" held at Arrowmont School in 1993. Notable exhibits are International Textile Competition at the Kyoto Art Museum, "Designs in Sculptural Fiber." "Natural Influence: A National Textile Review," "Contemporary American Surface Design" in Kyoto, a solo show at The Fine Arts Gallery, Texas Women's University, Denton, and "State of the Art: Contemporary Fiber" at Loveland Art Museum in Colorado.

KATHERINE WESTPHAL

Katherine Westphal has work in the permanent collections of the American Craft Museum, Renwick Gallery of The Smithsonian Institution, Trondheim (Norway) Museum, Rhode Island School of Design Museum, Arizona State University, University of Nebraska, the Hauberg Collection in Seattle, Washington, and many private collections. Recent invitational shows include "Frontiers in Fiber," "Craft Today," and "The New Narrative," and the premiere show at the Okun Gallery in Santa Fe. She had solo shows at the San Francisco Craft and Folk Art Museum, Museum of Contemporary Crafts in New York City, Fiberworks in Berkeley, California, Museum West in San Francisco, and the University of California at Davis. Her work can be seen at Mobilia, Cambridge, Massachusetts, Okun Gallery, Santa Fe, and The Sybaris Gallery, Royal Oak, Michigan. Westphal is professor of design emeritus from U.C.-Davis and lives in California with her husband, Ed Rossbach.

SUSAN WILCHINS, 4517 Keswick Dr., Raleigh, NC 27609

Susan Wilchins has an M.F.A. in Textile Design/Fiber Art from the University of Kansas. Her work has been exhibited in invitational shows throughout the United States, including "Energetic Fibers," "Fiber: Five Points of View," and "Perspectives from the Rim." Recent traveling shows with which she exhibited are "Southern Quilts: A New View," "Celebrating the Stitch," and "Arte Textil: Fibers USA/Columbia." Wilchins has curated a number of exhibits, received a 1991/92 Visual Artist Fellowship grant from the North Carolina Arts Council, and has been on the faculty at N.C. State University School of Design since 1982.

ERMA MARTIN YOST, 223 York St., Jersey City, NJ 07302

Represented by Noho Gallery in New York City, Erma Martin Yost was the 1992 recipient of an arts fellowship grant from the New Jersey State Council on the Arts. She has exhibited in many juried shows: "Mennonite Contemporary Artists," Goshen (Indiana) College; "Southwestern Exposure" at the Gayle Wilson Gallery, Southampton, New York; "The Insider As Outsider," Main/Access Gallery, Winnipeg, Manitoba, Canada; and "Quilt National '91," a traveling show. She has work in a number of permanent collections including the Port Authority at the World Trade Center in New York.

ACID DYE - One that benefits from, or requires, the addition of a chemical to control its union with fiber.

AIRBRUSH - An atomizer which utilizes compressed air to spray paint or other liquids.

"Airbrush technique is used to create repeat patterns. Though this is similar to what is done with screen print, the subtle color change that begins in one corner and ends in another, no matter what the pattern does, could not." - A. Nickolson

ALUM - Various white crystallines, especially aluminum potassium sulfate, used as a mordant.

ARASHI SHIBORI - Resist technique of Japan in which cloth is wrapped around a tapered pole, wound with thread, then compressed to one end of the pole before dyeing. There are a number of variations, including twisting the cloth as it is compressed, covering portions of the compressed cloth, using different weight thread, varying the pole diameter, and so on.

"Retaining the pleats by 'capturing' the process is one of the attractions of working with this technique." - A.L. Hedstrom

BATIK - Dye resist in which hot wax is applied to prevent the dye from penetrating the cloth. The cloth is then immersed in a cold-water bath.

"Brushes, tjantings, carved blocks, and found objects are used to apply the wax. A series of lines, calligraphic motions and scratches then build the structure of the surface." - D. Caldwell

BINDING - Dye resist in which a section of cloth is stretched taut, then thread is wound around it and tied off.

BLEACHOUT - See discharge.

BLOCK PRINTED - See batik and tjap.

CARRAGEEN - A cold-water moss. The insulating gum that coats it dissolves when it is boiled, thus thickening the surrounding liquid. Extract of the moss serves as a sizing agent in marbling.

CLAMP RESIST - Cloth is folded, then repeatedly reverse folded until it is a neat bundle. It is laid between boards, foam core or any stiff material, and tied with cords before being placed in a dye bath.

COCHINEAL DYES - Red dye obtained from the dried bodies of female cochineal (*Dactylopius coccus*) insects.

COLLAGE - A composition which consists of materials adhered to a surface.

COLORIST - Textile industry employee who renders new designs in different color combinations, usually for presentation to a client.

CYANOTYPE - Contact print technique. A light-sensitive emulsion is applied to the fabric, which is then dried in a darkroom. Positive or negative film is positioned on it and exposed to ultraviolet light to develop a blue image.

"I spent an entire summer in the darkroom teaching myself about cyanotype. I experimented with many types of fabric, colors of fabric, and with varying the concentration of the chemicals." - E. Yost

DIRECT DYE OR PAINT - Applying liquid or pigment paste to the cloth without using a resist.

DISCHARGE DYEING - Using a chemical agent to remove or diminish color from a previously dyed fabric.

FABRIC PAINT - Pigment paste with a consistency conducive to brushing

171

MICHAEL OLSZEWSKI USED ARASHI SHIBORI AND BATIK RESISTS AS WELL AS DIRECT DYE ON **NEED** (detail).

it onto the cloth. Can be made colorfast by applying heat.

FIBER REACTIVE DYE - A dye which bonds to the fiber. It is bright, has colorfastness, can be used for direct application or bath (vat) dyeing.

FILAMENT SILK - Silk which is loosely twisted as it is unwound from the coccoon in an unbroken strand.

FROTTAGE - Making an image by placing fabric or paper on a three-dimensional surface and brushing, daubing, or rubbing a color agent over the fabric or paper.

GOLD LEAF - See metal leaf.

GUTTA - A fluid latex, applied to fabric to prevent the flowing through or running of dyes or paints.

HABUTAI - Fine, paper-thin Chinese silk.

HAND - Indicates the flexibility and feel of fabric to the touch.

"When the dyed imagery was complete, I would heat set the dyes with an iron and then wash the piece. When the extra dye was removed, the fabric returned to a soft hand." - V.Z. Rivers

HAND PAINTED DYE - See direct dye.

HEAT SET - The application of heat to stabilize the color on newly dyed or painted fabric.

HEAT TRANSFER - Process in which an image on a specially coated paper is placed printed-side down on fabric and transferred to the fabric by the use of heat and pressure.

IKAT - Resist technique in which small bundles of yarn are tied off and dyed before weaving.

INDIGO - Dye originally obtained from the woad or indigo plants. Made synthetically since the early 1900s.

"Indigo blue is a complex, dense, compelling color that is always changing. Yet it is the power of indigo to connect and to be almost fundamental which is its essence." - A. Lindberg

INTERLACING - Weaving process done using relatively stiff materials. Since the tension of a loom is not necessary, it can be done by hand.

"My choice to experiment with contemporary materials led to the ancient technique of interlacing. The immediacy of this process led to the development of large-scale, mixed media wall pieces." - A. Sandoval

KATAGAMI - Stencil made from two to four layers of laminated handmade paper, used by the Japanese for applying resist paste.

KATAZOME - Japanese resist technique in which paste is applied with the aid of a stencil, usually prior to dip dyeing fabric.

KERMES - The dried bodies of the females of the scale insect genus *Kermes*, used as a red dye.

KINSAI - Gold powder. An adhesive is applied to the fabric and the powder is dusted onto it, usually with a tube having a fine-mesh screen.

KUMO SHIBORI - Dye resist technique in which precise portions of the fabric are pulled into narrow cone shapes. Thread is wound round each cone tightly, from base to tip, then tip to base. When the thread is removed after dyeing, a circular, spiderweb-like design is revealed.

"I went to a demonstration on shibori techniques. I was taken by the high contrast, intricate patterns and texture of the indigo-and-white cloth. Something clicked. This was the medium I had been looking for." - D. Beytebiere

LITHOGRAPH - Print made when an image is drawn on a stone or plate with a greasy crayon or ink. It is then chemically treated so the oily image attracts ink and the blank area rejects it.

LUREX - Plastic-coated metallic yarn developed by Dow Chemical.

MADDER ROOT - The root of the perennial vine, *rubia tinctorum*, from which a red dye can be extracted.

MARBLED - Process in which thickened paints are floated on water and manipulated to create a design. Fabric or paper is laid carefully on the surface and the design is transferred.

MARBLE DUST - See carrageen.

METAL LEAF - Gold, copper, or silver which has been beaten into extremely thin sheets.

"Processes related to traditional Japanese techniques are used to apply an adhesive, then impress the metal leaf into the surface of the fabric. This metal leaf application is a process that has been used for centuries and is still used to embellish fabric for kimono." - G. Kaufman

MONOTYPE - Print made by brushing ink or paint on a plate, then pressing paper on it to pick up the impression.

MORDANT - Substance that has an affinity for the dye and the fiber. It is the link which sets the color in the fabric.

"We entered a central courtyard. It was an open-air factory, the production area for the dyers and printers. Neatly folded lengths of off-white cloth were piled around the edges. The cloth was saturated with mordant." - K. Westphal, Introduction

MUREX - A gastropod of the genus *Murex trunculus* which is a source of royal purple dye.

MYLAR - Strong, flexible polyester film developed by E.I. DuPont Company.

OFFSET PRINTING - Process whereby an inked or painted image is made onto a vinyl- or rubber-blanketed cylinder, then transferred to fabric or paper by the use of pressure.

PASTE (RESIST) - Made of rice flour, bran, salt, and water. See katazome and yuzen.

PHOTO EMULSION - Thick light-sensitive liquid which hardens after it is exposed to ultraviolet light.

PHOTOGRAPHIC SCREEN PRINT - An image developed by incorporating light-sensitive film or emulsion to create the stencil for the printing process. See screen print.

"Personal photographs are incorporated in exploring the potential of altering images, with parts of various photographs often collaged together. A complex field is achieved by laying color, textures, and photographic images together in the process of printing." - C. Verstegen

POLE WRAPPING - A dye resist created by wrapping cloth around, then compressing it on, a cylinder. See arashi shibori.

POLYMER MEDIUM - Milky liquid or latex usually used as a dilutant. It is also used as an adhesive in collage, as a protective varnish for paintings and collage, and as a resist in dyeing.

RESIST - A technique or material which impedes dye or pigments from penetrating fabric. See batik, binding, clamp resist, gutta, ikat, katazome, roketsu-zome, shibori, stencil, stitch resist, tie-dye, yuzen.

ROKETSU-ZOME - Japanese resist technique utilizing a hot wax blend, probably introduced by the Chinese.

"Since roketsu is primarily brush-dyed, shading and color control are easily managed." - B. Benjamin

SCREEN PRINT - Image making technique in which a squeegee is used to force color medium through a tautly stretched mesh attached to a frame. Stencils are attached to the frame in order to block the medium, allowing it to pass only through the open areas to create the design.

"I enjoy the tension created between the initial impression that a work is elegant and the discovery that it is screen printed with words which are in opposition to that elegance." - J. Giordano

SERIGRAPHY - Using the silkscreen process to make a print, often with a cut stencil.

SHIBORI - A dye resist created by the manipulation of fabric. See arashi, binding, clamp resist, kumo, stitch resist, tie-dye.

SILVER LEAF - See metal leaf.

SODIUM ALGENATE - Gum extract of seaweed, used to thicken dye when more control of the dye is desired.

STENCIL - A thin, firm material from which a design has been cut. It is

173

MARY ANNE JORDAN'S
WHEAT & LADDER I
is screen printed, batiked, discharge dyed, and painted. Photo: Luke Jordan.

GLOSSARY

laid on another surface and paste pigment is passed over it to reproduce the design.

STITCH RESIST - Use of thread to make areas on the fabric which will not be affected by dyeing.

"Shapes are outlined or filled with running stitches. After the stitching is completed, the threads are drawn up tightly and tied securely. The fabric is entered into the dye bath until the desired color has been achieved. The fabric is rinsed, dried, and the stitches carefully removed. Further rinsing is usually required before finishing." - G. Kaufman

STYLIST - Textile industry creative director or consultant, responsible for the development of fabric designs.

TANNIN - Any of a variety of substances capable of promoting tanning.

TEXTILE PAINT - See fabric paint.

TIE-DYE - Resist in which the design is constructed using string, thread, yarn, or rubber bands to bind the fabric before dyeing.

TJANTING - A fountain-pen-like tool used to apply a hot wax dye resist. Traditionally, the body is bamboo, with a reservoir to hold the wax and a spout of copper or brass.

TJAP - A block or stamp used for wax resist application. Traditionally, the tool is carved, engraved, or made of a combination of copper strips and nails embedded in wood.

WARP PAINT OR PRINT - To paint or print on the threads which run the length (vertical) of the cloth before weaving, but as it is on the loom. This adds an indistinct design when the intersecting (weft) threads are introduced.

"Imagery is painted on the warp in the same manner as the 1920s Japanese pictorial warp-print ikat, hogushi-ori, which was stencilled. A contemporary interpretation can be achieved on a computer-assisted loom." - J.S. Pollack

WAX RESIST - See batik.

WOAD - The plant *Isatis tinctoria.* Its leaves yield a blue dye.

XEROX TRANSFER - The image is copied onto a resin-coated paper. Application of heat causes it to adhere to another surface.

YUZEN - Japanese dye painting technique. Paste resist is applied with a cone-shaped applicator or, through stencils, the dye is brushed onto the fabric.

174

RELATED READING

Barber, E.J.W. *Prehistoric Textiles: The Development of Cloth in the Neolithic and Bronze Ages.* Princeton, NJ: Princeton University Press, 1991. Cited on pp. 6-8, 19, 25, 37, 43, 47, 53, 59, 65, 69, 73, 77, 91, 97, 101, 107, 113, 119, 125, 129, 133, 139, 145, 151, 155, 159, 165.

Bristow, Nicholas. *Screen Printing: Design & Technique.* London, England: B.T. Batsford Ltd., 1991.

Buchanan, Rita. *A Weaver's Garden.* Loveland, CO: Interweave Press, 1987.

Colchester, Chloe. *The New Textiles.* New York, NY: Rizzoli International, 1991.

Dyrenforth, Noel. *The Technique of Batik.* Avon, Great Britain: The Bath Press, 1988.

Elliott, Inger McCabe. *Batik, Fabled Cloth of Java.* New York, NY: Clarkson N. Potter, Inc., 1984. Cited on p. 7 and 31.

FIBERARTS: The Magazine of Textiles. Edited by Ann Batchelder. Asheville, NC: Altamont Press. Jan/Feb 1989, Mar/Apr 1992, Sep/Oct 1992, Mar/Apr 1993.

The Illustrated History of Textiles. Edited by Madeleine Ginsberg. New York, NY: Portland House/Random House, 1991.

Johnston, Ann. *Dye Painting!* Paducah, KY: American Quilter's Society, 1992.

Kaufman, Glen and Meda Parker Johnston. *Design on Fabrics.* New York, NY: Van Nostrand Reinhold, 1981.

Nettles, Bea. *Breaking the Rules: A Photo Media Cookbook.* Urbana, IL: Inky Press, 1987.

Osma, Guillermo de. *Mariano Fortuny: His Life and Work.* New York, NY: Rizzoli International, 1980.

Proctor, Richard M. and Jennifer F. Lew. *Surface Design For Fabric.* Seattle, WA: University of Washington Press, 1984.

Robinson, Stuart. *A History of Dyed Textiles.* Cambridge, MA: M.I.T. Press, 1969. Cited on p. 83.

Stocksdale, Joy. *Polychromatic Screen Printing.* Berkeley, CA: Oregon Street Press, 1984.

Surface Design Journal. Edited by Charles Talley. Oakland, CA: Surface Design Association.

Taylor, Carol. *The Great T-Shirt Book.* New York, NY: Sterling Publishing Co., 1992.

_____. *Marbling Paper & Fabric.* New York, NY: Sterling Publishing Co., 1991.

Wada, Yoshiko, Mary Kellogg Rice and Jane Barton. *Shibori: The Inventive Art of Japanese Shaped Resist Dyeing.* New York, NY: Kodansha International, Ltd., 1983.

ACKNOWLEDGEMENTS

THANKS:

To those who served as resources: Astrid Bennett, Sandra Blain, Lou Cabeen, Gerhardt Knodel, Cynthia Laymon, Patricia Malarcher, Pamela Scheinman, Charles Talley, Maria Tulokas, Yoshiko Wada, and James Wilson. A special thanks to Clare Verstegen for verifying the glossary, to Ann Batchelder, Rob Pulleyn and Carol Taylor for all their help, and to Chris Colando for his concerned, creative design.

PHOTOGRAPHY:

(Page)
(18) Cynthia Huff; (24) Mitchell Brauner; (30) Kaplan; (36) Gary Sutton; (42) Barry Shapiro; (46) Leon C. Yost; (47-51) Courtesy of Noho Gallery, NYC; (52) Richard Emery Nickolson; (58) Thomas Moore; (64) Chris Fladseth; (68-71) Eleanor Erskine; (76) Kanesaki Studio; (82) Robert di Franco; (90-95) John Griebsch; (96) Victor Marshall; (100) Bill Helwig; (106) Al Surratt; (112) Bill Woods; (118-123) Marc Wilchins; (124) Alan Watson; (128-131) Roger Clayden; (132) Ron Erickson; (138) Janet Century; (144) Bryan Buyla; (145-149) Mary S. Rezny; (150) Lisa Hermanson; (154) Tina Cassara; (158-163) Luke Jordan; (164) Cylla Von Tiedemann.

INDEX 175

INDEX

176